MURDER ON THE TRAIN

MURDER ON THE TRAIN

A MISCARRIAGE OF JUSTICE IN EDWARDIAN NORTHUMBERLAND

~ JOHN J. EDDLESTON ~

PEN & SWORD
TRUE CRIME

First published in Great Britain in 2025 by
PEN AND SWORD TRUE CRIME
An imprint of
Pen & Sword Books Limited
Yorkshire – Philadelphia

Copyright © John J. Eddleston, 2025

ISBN 978 1 03612 492 2

The right of John J. Eddleston to be identified as Author of this work has been asserted by him in accordance with the Copyright, Designs and Patents Act 1988.

A CIP catalogue record for this book is available from the British Library.

All rights reserved. No part of this book may be reproduced, transmitted, downloaded, decompiled or reverse engineered in any form or by any means, electronic or mechanical including photocopying, recording or by any information storage and retrieval system, without permission from the Publisher in writing. NO AI TRAINING: Without in any way limiting the Author's and Publisher's exclusive rights under copyright, any use of this publication to "train" generative artificial intelligence (AI) technologies to generate text is expressly prohibited. The Author and Publisher reserve all rights to license uses of this work for generative AI training and development of machine learning language models.

Typeset in Times New Roman 12/16 by SJmagic DESIGN SERVICES, India.
Printed and bound in the UK by CPI Group (UK) Ltd.

The Publisher's authorised representative in the EU for product safety is Authorised Rep Compliance Ltd., Ground Floor, 71 Lower Baggot Street, Dublin D02 P593, Ireland.
www.arccompliance.com

For a complete list of Pen & Sword titles please contact
PEN & SWORD BOOKS LIMITED
George House, Units 12 & 13, Beevor Street, Off Pontefract Road,
Barnsley, South Yorkshire, S71 1HN, England
E-mail: enquiries@pen-and-sword.co.uk
Website: www.pen-and-sword.co.uk

or

PEN AND SWORD BOOKS
1950 Lawrence Rd, Havertown, PA 19083, USA
E-mail: uspen-and-sword@casematepublishers.com
Website: www.penandswordbooks.com

Contents

Introduction.. vii

Section One: The Events of 1910

Chapter 1 Friday, 18 March 1910.. 2
Chapter 2 John Innes Nisbet... 8
Chapter 3 Saturday, 19 March to Sunday, 20 March 1910......... 11
Chapter 4 John Alexander Dickman.. 17
Chapter 5 Monday, 21 March 1910.. 20
Chapter 6 Tuesday, 22 March to Sunday, 3 April 1910.............. 24
Chapter 7 Monday, 4 April to Wednesday, 13 April 1910.......... 28
Chapter 8 Thursday, 14 April to Friday, 15 April 1910.............. 30
Chapter 9 Saturday, 16 April to Wednesday, 8 June 1910......... 35
Chapter 10 Thursday, 9 June 1910... 37
Chapter 11 Friday, 10 June to Sunday, 3 July 1910.................... 41
Chapter 12 Monday, 4 July 1910 – Early Witnesses................... 43
Chapter 13 Monday, 4 July 1910 – Identifications..................... 46
Chapter 14 Monday, 4 July 1910 – Later Witnesses................... 53
Chapter 15 Tuesday, 5 July 1910 – The Final Witnesses............ 57
Chapter 16 Tuesday, 5 July 1910 – Dickman's Evidence............ 62
Chapter 17 Tuesday, 5 July 1910 – Cross Examination.............. 68
Chapter 18 Tuesday, 5 July 1910 – Summation.......................... 73
Chapter 19 Wednesday, 6 July 1910... 76
Chapter 20 Thursday, 7 July to Thursday, 21 July 1910............. 81

Chapter 21 Friday, 22 July 1910 87
Chapter 22 Saturday, 23 July to Monday, 8 August 1910 92
Chapter 23 Tuesday, 9 August 1910 98

Section Two: The Evidence Reviewed

Chapter 24 If John Alexander Dickman Were Guilty 102
Chapter 25 The Evidence Against John Alexander Dickman 108
Chapter 26 The Identification Evidence 111
Chapter 27 Dickman's Financial Problems 118
Chapter 28 The Isabella Pit Shaft 124
Chapter 29 The Firearms Evidence 127
Chapter 30 The Staining Evidence 135
Chapter 31 The Remaining Evidence 138
Chapter 32 Bogus Information and a Confession 141
Chapter 33 If Dickman Were Innocent 151

Section Three: Two Other Murders

Chapter 34 The Murder of Caroline Luard 156
Chapter 35 The Murder of Herman Cohen 163

Section Four: An Alternate Solution

Chapter 36 A Review 170
Chapter 37 The Murder of John Innes Nisbet 175
Chapter 38 Justice 186

Index 189

Introduction

In the spring of 1910, a brutal murder took place on a train in the Newcastle-upon-Tyne area. John Innes Nisbet, a mild-mannered, slightly built man was shot in the head five times and the colliery wage bag he had been carrying was stolen.

A few days after the crime, John Alexander Dickman, a man who earned his living taking bets, was arrested and charged with murder. He faced his trial in July, and was convicted on purely circumstantial evidence. Despite the fact that at least one police officer had assisted a witness in identifying the prisoner, the sentence was upheld at the Court of Appeal, and Dickman went to the gallows, protesting that he was an innocent man.

This book puts forward an argument that Dickman was indeed innocent. It examines all the various strands of evidence, used to convict Dickman, and shows that his conviction was unsafe.

It then goes on to construct a stronger case against someone else and, after more than 100 years, outlines what might really have happened.

Section One

THE EVENTS OF 1910

Chapter 1

Friday, 18 March 1910

At 12.06pm, on Friday, 18 March 1910, the 10.27am train from Newcastle Central station arrived at Alnmouth. (*See Plate 1*).

The train was on time but had to pull in at a different platform than it would usually have done. The reason for this was that an express behind it was running late, and that was to be given priority. By having the Newcastle train wait on a different platform, the express would be able to thunder through the station without any further delay. This meant, of course, that anyone entering or leaving any of the carriages of the Newcastle train would be doing so at the opposite side from all those who had travelled thus far.

Thomas William Charlton, was a foreman porter at Alnmouth and as he went about his duties, the first of the four carriages, the one nearest the engine, caught his eye. In one of the four compartments of that carriage, someone had left a window open. Charlton went to close it.

Immediately he opened the door, Charlton could see that something was terribly wrong. Three streams of blood had spread themselves across the floor of the compartment and they all seemed to be emanating from beneath the left hand seat at the far side of the carriage.

Gingerly, Charlton stepped inside the third-class compartment and investigated. He found, to his horror, that a man's body had been jammed beneath the seat furthest from the engine. All the blood originated in the region of the man's head, which lay at the farthest side from the platform. Beside the man's head lay a hard, felt hat and

Friday, 18 March 1910

close by a pair of gold-rimmed spectacles, broken into two pieces. One of the lenses was missing and Charlton now saw that it lay on the arm rest closest to the platform, almost directly over where the man's feet lay.

Without waiting to see what condition the poor man might be in, Charlton ran for assistance, calling a porter, the stationmaster and the train's guard. Robert Wilkinson was the guard and he had joined the train at Newcastle Central, travelling in the last of the four carriages. The train had called at fifteen stations between Newcastle and Alnmouth, the busiest of which was Morpeth, but Wilkinson had not seen or heard anything suspicious during the journey.

The first police officer on the scene was Constable George Nisbet. He made a cursory search of the compartment and discovered that the hat found close to the victim's head had a name-tag inside it. This read, 'J.I. Nisbet, 180, Heaton Road, Heaton'. It seemed that by coincidence, the dead man bore the same surname as the constable. Other items were also found inside the compartment including two newspapers and a return ticket to Widdrington, one of the stations between Morpeth and Alnmouth. There was also a heavily bloodstained glove lying on the floor. It was clear that this belonged to the dead man as a matching glove was still on his hand. Constable Nisbet also found a bullet on the floor. The victim had clearly been shot dead.

At around 2.00pm, Doctor Charles Clarke Burnham, the police surgeon for Alnwick arrived. He pronounced life extinct and noticed a number of wounds, all in the dead man's head. It seemed that the man had been shot at least three or four times.

At about the same time, Superintendent Bolton had arrived to take charge of the investigation. He watched as Constable Nisbet made a more careful search of the compartment. In all, four bullets would eventually be discovered and, since these were of two different calibres, it seemed obvious that two weapons had been used and this implied two assailants. The police immediately deduced that they were looking for at least two desperate attackers.

The name and address printed in the hat band found in the carriage caused further investigations to be made back in Newcastle. These revealed that the dead man's full name was John Innes Nisbet. Nisbet had been born on 13 January 1866, which meant that he had been 44 years old when he died. In January 1893, shortly after his 27th birthday, he had married Cicely Elizabeth Waterson. The couple had had two children, both girls, Cicely Gertrude and Lily.

Police enquiries at Nisbet's home in Heaton and an interview with his distraught wife revealed that ever since he had left school, John Innes Nisbet had worked for Messrs Rayne and Burn, colliery owners, who had offices based in Beaconsfield Chambers, Sandhill, Newcastle. For the past twenty years or so, part of Nisbet's duty, on a fortnightly basis, had been to take the wages for the men who worked at the Stobswood colliery. On the day of his death, Nisbet had been carrying out this task and should have alighted from the train at Widdrington, the closest station to the colliery. This immediately narrowed down the location of the murder since it must obviously have taken place before that station.

Cicely Nisbet also revealed that on these fortnightly journeys she was in the habit of walking down to Heaton station, which wasn't far from her home, to meet her husband's train when it pulled in at 10.34am. They would exchange a few words during the minute or so that the train was in the station and then Cicely would walk home and await John's return after his work was over.

Things had been no different on 18 March. Cicely had been waiting at Heaton station (*see Plate 2*), but when the train pulled in she could see no sign of her husband. Normally he travelled at the back of the train but as she looked along the platform she suddenly saw him leaning out of a window at the front end. Cicely ran along the platform and managed to exchange just a few words with John before the train pulled slowly away. During that time she managed to see that there was another man in John's compartment. He was sitting on the far side of the carriage with his back to the engine, but

Friday, 18 March 1910

she could offer no description of him as he had his collar pulled up and he was enveloped in a deep shadow cast from a nearby bridge (*see Plate 3*). Still, at least the police now knew that Nisbet was alive and well at Heaton.

Enquiries at Nisbet's employer, Rayne and Burn, revealed that Thomas Anderson, the cashier and manager of the offices, had that morning handed a cheque for £370 9s 6d to Nisbet, along with a lockable black leather bag, which was some nine inches in length. That cheque had been presented by Nisbet, at around 10.00am, at Lloyds Bank, where a clerk, John Bradshaw Wilson, had handed over £231 in sovereigns, £103 in half-sovereigns, £35 9s in silver and £1 0s 6d in copper.

The gold had been in three canvas bank bags, the silver in paper bags and the copper in a brown paper parcel. These had all been placed inside the lockable black leather bag but no such bag had been found in the railway carriage so the motive for the crime seemed to be obvious. Nisbet had been brutally murdered for the cash he was carrying and it was now clear that the crime must have taken place between Heaton and Widdrington.

That same afternoon and evening, reports of the crime appeared in the local press. Already speculation was that this was the work of a gang, rather than an individual assailant, especially since the victim had been shot a number of times and with bullets of two different calibres. However, further crucial information was about to be revealed.

Percival Harding Hall and John William Spink were also clerks for a local colliery company. They worked for the Netherton Coal Company, which had offices at Cathedral Buildings in Dean Street, Newcastle and on 18 March, they had been on a similar errand to Nisbet and had travelled by the same train. Having heard reports of the crime, they came forward that same afternoon to say what they had seen.

Hall, apparently the more useful of these two witnesses, stated that they had made the same journey as Nisbet, on alternate Fridays, for a number of years and knew him well by sight. That morning, they had taken their seats in a compartment in the front carriage of the train. Their compartment was the second one in that first carriage.

Spink had made himself comfortable, but Hall had decided to look out of the window. As he did so, he saw Nisbet coming along the platform towards him, in the company of another man. The two were in conversation and Hall heard Nisbet say, 'We will make this a smoker.' The companion walked on to the first compartment and shouted back 'This one's a smoker' but by now Nisbet was already inside the first compartment and the other man returned to join him. Hall was able to give a reasonably detailed description of Nisbet's companion and said he would be able to pick the man out of a dozen.

The train left Newcastle Central on time and a few minutes later, as it pulled into Heaton, Hall was again looking out of the carriage window and saw a woman, Mrs Nisbet, running along the platform to exchange a few words with her husband. Hall heard her say something about being home by 6.00pm.

In due course, the train arrived at Stannington where Hall and Spink alighted (*see Plate 4*). As they waited for the train to pull out they stood on the platform and both men saw Nisbet in the next compartment and nodded to him. Nisbet was sitting on the far side of the compartment, facing the engine and he had a companion, sitting opposite to him with his back to the engine and from the description Spink furnished, it might well have been the same man that Hall had seen with Nisbet at Newcastle.

Those newspapers reports also brought forward another witness. Charles Raven was a commercial traveller, living in King John Terrace, Newcastle. Raven came forward on the Friday evening and said that he had known the dead man, by sight, for some five or six years. Raven had not known Nisbet's name, but had spoken to him from time to time.

That morning, Raven had been at the Central station. It was around 10.20am that he was walking towards platform 4 from the

Friday, 18 March 1910

west side of the station. When he was only a few yards from the gate he saw Nisbet apparently walking with another man. The two men walked through the gate to platform 4 and turned to the right, heading towards platform 5, from where the 10.27 train departed. He added that the two men were not in conversation.

As 18 March drew to a close, the police had accepted that John Innes Nisbet had been brutally murdered for the cash he carried. The location of the crime had been narrowed down to somewhere between Stannington and Widdrington. Finally, they also believed that they had a decent description of one of the men who may have committed the crime, possibly as a member of a gang.

Chapter 2

John Innes Nisbet

The problem with tracing the history of the man who had been so brutally killed is that his somewhat unusual name caused all sorts of problems for census takers and other officials. Those officials made mistakes on his marriage certificate and on the last census taken before his death, that of 1901. Be that as it may, it has been possible to determine some of the history of the murdered man (*see Plate 5*).

John Innes Nisbet was born on 13 January 1866, at Quayside in Newcastle, confirming that he was 44 years old when he died. His father's name is given as David Mein Nisbet, and his mother as Mary Walker Nisbet, née Innes. The father's occupation is given as a Post Office clerk and their registered address was 43 Carliol Street, also in Newcastle, and close to the prison.

There had already been, by the time John was born, some family tragedy. In the 1851 census, although again the surname was listed incorrectly, David and Mary Nisbet were living at 90 Gosforth Avenue, in Haworth, County Durham, and his occupation is given as a house carpenter. At the time they had two children: a 6-year-old son named Alexander and a 3-year-old daughter, Lily. Ten years later however, at the time of the 1861 census, David and Mary had moved to 17 St John Street in the Westgate area of Newcastle. By now, David has taken up his position with the Post Office and is listed as a letter carrier, but there is no mention of the children. By this time, Alexander would have been 16 and Lily just 13.

In fact, there is evidence that both children had died. The death of an 'Alexander Nesbit [sic]' is recorded in Berwick in December

1853, and the death of a 'Lilly [sic] Elizabeth Nisbet' is recorded in Newcastle-upon-Tyne in June 1856.

At the time of the 1871 census, John Innes Nisbet was 5 years old. Once again the census taker failed to note the surname correctly and the family are listed as Nesbett. John's father is now a bank porter and the family live at 9 Side, Newcastle.

Just eight years later, on 21 October 1879, David Mein Nisbet died, leaving John alone with his mother. Two years after this, during the 1881 census, we find Mary and John, who by now is aged 15, living at 4 Wardle Terrace in Newcastle. The house is shared with Janet Smith, a 15-year-old boarder, Catherine Brown, a servant and Robert Stirling, a lodger.

Further tragedy followed the next year when, in early 1882, John's mother Mary died. John now becomes a lodger with another family and soon afterwards, at the age of about 16, he takes up employment with the only company he would ever work for, Messrs Rayne and Burn, colliery owners.

The next census took place in 1891 and John was then listed as a lodger at 12 Warwick Street in Heaton with the Birkley family. Two years later, on 26 January 1893, John married Cicely Elizabeth Waterson, who was four years his junior. At the time of his marriage, John was living at 48 Walker Terrace, in Gateshead. Soon, however, the newlyweds move to 77 South View West and their first child, a daughter named Cicely Gertrude was born that same year.

By 1897, John and his family are living at 14 King John Terrace. Two years later, in 1899, a second daughter, Lily, is born, possibly named in remembrance of John's deceased sister. By the following year, 1900, the family have moved back to South View West, but are now living at number 80. They are still there at the time of the next census, in 1901. Once again his surname is incorrectly recorded, this time as Nesbitt. His occupation is also erroneously listed as a granary bookkeeper.

Sometime in 1902, the family move again, this time to 7 Fifth Avenue. They live there for a few years but in 1909, they move for the final time, to 180 Heaton Road, Heaton, where John was living at the time of his death.

Dying in 1910, John would never know what happened to the three female members of his family that he left behind. He would not know that in 1913, his widow would marry one Robert Foster Meikle and that they would emigrate to Victoria, British Columbia, in Canada. They would have one daughter whom they would name Yvonne. Robert and Cicely took Nisbet's two daughters with them to Canada and it was there that the two sisters married two brothers. Cicely Gertrude married Arthur Danby whilst Lily married Montague Danby. Their descendants still live in British Columbia.

Chapter 3

Saturday, 19 March to Sunday, 20 March 1910

We have already seen that by the end of Friday, 18 March, the officers investigating the murder of John Innes Nisbet had been able to narrow down the location of the murder as having occurred somewhere between Stannington and Widdrington stations.

The evidence of the two cashiers, Hall and Spink, showed that Nisbet was still alive at Stannington but, since he hadn't alighted from the train at his designated stop, Widdrington, he must have been dead by the time the train reached that station. This, however, did not help a great deal (*see Plate 6*).

The information the police had thus far, meant that Nisbet could have been killed as early as 11.06am or as late as 11.31am. That was not only a twenty-five minute window, but it also covered five railway stations. It had to be narrowed down even more, if possible. Fortunately, a witness came forward who would be able to do just that.

John Grant was a platelayer and on 18 March he was on Morpeth station, waiting for the Newcastle train to arrive, so that he could travel to Longhirst. Grant was at the top end of the platform, close to where the engine stopped. He then started to walk down the length of the train, looking for a suitable, smoking compartment.

As he walked along the first carriage, he casually looked into the compartments. As he looked into the third compartment, the one in which Nisbet had been seen at the previous stop, Grant noticed that it was empty. He swore that had there been anyone in that compartment,

11

he would have seen them. Grant was certainly observant for he did notice a gentleman named Andrew Bruce in the first compartment. Eventually, Grant climbed into the first compartment of the second carriage, which was a smoking compartment.

Grant's testimony was important for two reasons; one of which the police immediately seized on, one of which they would later completely ignore.

The first point is that by the time the train arrived at Morpeth, the compartment in which Nisbet had been seen at Stannington, and in which his body would later be found at Alnmouth, was apparently empty. The only possible explanation is that Nisbet was already dead and his body stuffed beneath the seat. He must, therefore, have been murdered between Stannington and Morpeth. The time of his death was thus greatly narrowed down, as was the possible location.

The second point was of equal import. Grant did not see anyone get out of the murder compartment at Morpeth. Yet, according to the testimony of Hall and Spink, there had been another man in that compartment at the previous stop, Stannington. The inference was, of course, that this companion must have been the man who killed Nisbet and the only way he would have avoided detection by the observant Grant was to have leapt from the train between the two stations. At this stage, there was no suggestion that the killer, whoever he was, had alighted from the train at Morpeth. The police were already accepting that the killer must have jumped from the train and, indeed, a thorough search of the track between Stannington and Morpeth was put into place.

The story of the murder made headlines and a great deal of copy, not only in the Newcastle newspapers, but also in others throughout the region. The story of the crime was told and the description given by Hall was circulated. The description was rather vague but detailed a man who was 'About 35 to 40, about 5ft 6ins tall, about eleven stone, medium build, dark moustache,

Saturday, 19 March to Sunday, 20 March 1910

pale or sallow complexion; wore a light overcoat down to his knees; black hard felt hat; well dressed and appeared to be fairly well to do.'

The newspapers also carried a statement made by the man who had found the body, the porter, Thomas William Charlton. He stated,

> When the 10.27 train from Newcastle arrived at Alnmouth at 12.08 I was commencing to collect tickets in the train. I saw a window down in one of the compartments, which was apparently empty.
>
> I opened the door to put the window up, when I noticed a lot of blood on the floor, oozing out from one of the corners. I looked under the seat and saw a man's body lying face downward and pushed right in under the seat. There were heating pipes under the seat opposite, but not under the seat where the body was.
>
> I at once understood that something serious had happened and found that the man was dead. I called the station manager who came and examined the compartment. We found blood on the cushions and a pair of spectacles, broken into several pieces, scattered all over.
>
> There were several bullet wounds on the man's head – one over the eye, another behind the ear, and another about the nose. His face was very badly disfigured. Later the body was removed from the carriage, which was detached and shunted.

The police, meanwhile, were exploring every possibility. Gun sellers in Newcastle were visited to trace recent purchases of a revolver. There were reports that a man had been seen, carrying a bank bag similar to the missing one, and walking about a mile and a half away from Morpeth station.

By now, the post-mortem had been carried out and this confirmed that two calibres of bullet had been used. Four bullets had been recovered: two leaden ones of .320 calibre had been found, and two nickel-plated ones of .250 calibre. Those bullets had caused a total of five wounds, all in Nisbet's head.

There were rumours that the killer might well have escaped to London. Apparently a man had been seen in the capital, spending gold freely and drinking whisky from a bottle labelled with the name of a Newcastle hotel. In the event he was traced and eliminated, being only an enthusiastic football supporter who had travelled to London to watch Newcastle United play Tottenham, a match which Newcastle won 4-0.

Andrew Bruce, the man who had been seen travelling in the first compartment of the murder carriage confirmed that he had been on the train, and had travelled from Newcastle to Alnmouth. There had been another man in his compartment, but he had left the train at Chevington. Bruce also confirmed that he had seen two clerks getting out at Stannington and, as they stood on the platform he saw them nod to someone on the train.

By now, Cicely Nisbet, the widow, had elaborated on her initial testimony and had given a full statement to the police. This began;

> I live at 180 Heaton Road, Newcastle. I have been married nearly eighteen years. The deceased, my husband, has been employed by Messrs Rayne and Burn, owners of the Stobswood colliery for twenty eight years.
>
> During the whole of our married life my husband went, on alternate Fridays, to Stobswood colliery to pay the workmen's wages. He always travelled to Widdrington station by the 10.27 train from Central station.
>
> It has been my invariable custom, unless prevented by illness, to be at Heaton station when the train passed

Saturday, 19 March to Sunday, 20 March 1910

through, to speak to my husband. He generally travelled in the rear or middle portion of the train.

About 10.30am on Friday, March 18th, I was upon the Heaton station platform on the arrival of the 10.27 train. I was standing in my usual position when the train stopped. I did not see my husband until I had glanced right along the carriages and was surprised to see him looking out of the window of a carriage near the engine. It would be either the second or third compartment from the engine.

I ran along the platform to him. My husband was laughing and appeared to be in excellent spirits. I had only time to say to him; 'You won't be later than six o'clock tonight mind, auntie is coming.' He replied; 'No, I will come straight home after I have been at the office.' The train was then on the move, and he pushed the carriage window up and sat down facing the engine.

I saw there was another man in the compartment but I can give no description whatever of him, as I only had a momentary glance at him. I observed a young man looking out of the compartment in front of the one containing my husband.

It seemed that the investigation was going nowhere fast. The police now knew that Nisbet had been murdered between Stannington and Morpeth, and had a description of a man seen with Nisbet but finding that man was a different manner. By Sunday morning they were no nearer the killer but then, a single telephone call gave them a name.

Wilson Hepple was a local artist, living near Acklington, but with a studio at 7 Gallowgate, Newcastle. He told the police that he had also travelled on the 10.27am train and, before it had left, had spent some time pacing up and down the platform outside his chosen carriage. As he paced, he saw two men walking towards him, heading towards the top of the train. From reading the newspaper reports, Hepple was certain that one of the men, the slighter of the two, was Nisbet.

This, of course, meshed with the testimony of Percival Harding Hall and Charles Raven, but Hepple could supply something of more value than a mere description of Nisbet's apparent companion. That companion was someone Hepple had known for many years and he was able to supply the police with a name. That name was John Alexander Dickman.

Chapter 4

John Alexander Dickman

No photograph exists of the man whose name had been given to the police. The only image we have is one drawn by a court reporter, later in the year 1910 (*see Plate 7*).

John Alexander Dickman was born on 17 May 1864 at 3 Marlborough Street, in the Westgate area of the street, close to the cattle market. This is unsurprising, as his father, Joseph, was a master butcher.

His mother, Zelina Catherine (née Royer) was French and, at the time of John's birth, was 29 years old.

Dickman was the third child born to Joseph and Zelina. Marie Rose had been born in 1860 and William had been born on 9 July 1862. William would, in later life, follow his father into the butchery trade.

In some ways, the life of John Dickman would parallel that of John Nisbet for it too would involve a degree of tragedy. When John Dickman was just 3 years old his mother found herself pregnant again. Unfortunately, there were complications. She gave birth to a son, who they named Joseph after his father, but neither the child nor the mother survived. Both Zelina and her new born child died in the year 1867, Zelina passing away on Valentine's Day, 14 February.

Joseph Dickman was now 34 years old and had three young children to look after, the eldest being just 7 years of age. He also had a business to run. Unable to cope by himself, Joseph took his family and moved in with his married sister, Jane Cooper, who lived in Whickham, and they are recorded there on the 1871 census. At the same time, Wilson Hepple, the artist who would give John Dickman's name to the police in 1910, was also living in Whickham, and it was at this time that the two first got to know each other.

Joseph did not stay with his sister for very long. Soon he moved in with his brother, also a master butcher, at 1 Front Street, Great Lumley. The family were living there at the time of the 1881 census, by which time John Alexander Dickman was almost 17.

Although he started off in the butchery business, dealing in meat was not to John's liking and he soon went into the mining industry instead, becoming a clerk for one colliery and later negotiating its sale, for which he received a handsome commission. A few years later he obtained a legacy from a deceased relative and decided to go into business for himself as a turf accountant. It wasn't perhaps, the most salubrious of businesses and it is likely that this caused some friction between John and his siblings. It is certain that his relationship with his elder brother William cooled somewhat and, in later years, would lead to a great deal of animosity.

In the year 1891, John's brother married one Annie Isabella Brown. Eventually the couple would go on to have five children: Zelina born in 1893, Thomas born in 1895, Joseph born in 1897, Mary born in 1899 and finally William, born in 1900. That same year, 1891, saw John Dickman living at 130 New Bridge Street.

John was still at that address the following year when, on 5 September 1892 he married Annie Sowerby Bainbridge, at St Nicholas' Cathedral. Again his life paralleled that of John Innes Nisbet for Dickman was also to father two children. A daughter, Catherine was born on 11 June 1893 at 45 Seventh Avenue and a son, Henry Royer Dickman, was born on 17 April 1897 at 97 Falmouth Road.

By the time of the 1901 census, the four members of the Dickman family were living at 11 Rothbury Terrace, but around 1907, they moved to 1 Lily Avenue, in Jesmond, and were still at that address in 1910 at the time of the murder of John Nisbet.

John Alexander Dickman

Though we are getting ahead of ourselves, the year 1910 would be the last year that John Dickman saw his family and, like Nisbet, he would never know what would happen to them.

Dickman's wife, Annie, would never remarry and stayed in the Newcastle area. She never changed her name and remained, proudly, as Annie Dickman until the day she died. Dickman's daughter, Catherine, never married and would be a force in the votes for women campaign. His son, Henry, would serve with distinction in the Great War and would marry twice, once in 1924 and again in 1939. There would be no children from his first marriage but the second would bear him two daughters and a son.

The descendants of John Alexander Dickman still live in England.

Chapter 5

Monday, 21 March 1910

The telephone call from Wilson Hepple had given the police the name of John Alexander Dickman. The task of investigating Dickman was given to Detective Inspector Andrew Tait and he spent most of Sunday the 20th and Monday the 21st looking into the history of his man. Tait's initial investigation seemed to indicate that Dickman might possibly have financial problems, which would certainly give him a motive for the crime.

On the Monday afternoon, Tait reported his findings to his superior, Superintendent John Weddell and was told to bring Dickman in for interview. So, at around 4.35pm on 21 March, Tait arrived at Dickman's home, 1 Lily Avenue.

Tait rang the doorbell and after a few seconds, it was Dickman himself who came to the door. 'Are you Mr Dickman?' asked Tait, and Dickman replied, 'Yes.'

'John Alexander Dickman?'

'Yes.'

'Were you at one time employed as a bookkeeper with a firm of shipbrokers in this city?'

'Yes.'

Tait then identified himself as a police officer and continued, 'The Northumberland County Police have been informed that you were

Monday, 21 March 1910

seen in the company of the murdered man Nisbet on Friday morning last. I have since learned that you were an acquaintance of his. If that is so, the county police would like to know if you could throw any light on the affair.'

Dickman did not seem nervous and answered: 'I knew Nisbet for many years. I saw him that morning. I booked at the ticket window with him, and went by the same train, but I did not see him after the train left. I would have told the police if I had thought it would do any good.'

Tait then asked Dickman if he would accompany him to the police office to see Superintendent Weddell and make a statement. Dickman said he would, without hesitation. He then went back into his house, followed by Tait, took off his slippers and put on his boots. The two men then left Lily Avenue to walk to Gosforth police station, with Dickman telling his wife that he wouldn't be long (*see Plate 8*).

In the Gosforth detective office, Dickman was seen by Weddell and freely made a statement detailing his movements on Friday, 18 March.

The statement began,

> On Friday morning last I went to the Central station and took a ticket, a return for Stannington. Nisbet, the deceased man, whom I knew, was at the ticket office before me, and, so far as I know, had left the hall by the time I got round.
>
> I went to the bookstall and got a paper, the *Manchester Sporting Chronicle*; then to the refreshment room, and had a pie and a glass of ale. I then went on to the platform and took my seat in a third-class compartment nearer the hinder end than the front end. My recollection is, although I am not clear on the matter, that people entered and left the compartment at different stations on the journey.

The train passed Stannington station without my noticing it, and I got out at Morpeth, and handed my ticket with excess fare, two and a half pence, to the collector. I left Morpeth and walked to Stannington by the main road. I took ill of diarrhoea on the way, and had to return to Morpeth, to catch the 1.12pm train, but missed it, and got the 1.40 slow at Morpeth.

After missing the 1.12pm I came out of the station at the east side, and turned down towards the town. I met a man named Elliott, and spoke to him. I did not get into the town, but turned and went back to the station, and got the 1.40pm slow to Newcastle. I got a single ticket for Stannington, and did not give it up. I gave up the return portion at the Manors.

I have been very unwell since, but was out on Saturday afternoon and evening. I went on the journey to see a Mr Hogg, at Dovecot, in connection with a new sinking operation there.

After making this statement, which Weddell wrote down and Dickman then signed as being accurate, he was asked to turn out his pockets. The sum of £17 9s 11d in cash was found, partly made up by fifteen sovereigns in a Lambton's Bank bag. The remainder of the cash was loose in Dickman's trouser pocket and consisted of one sovereign, two half sovereigns, one half crown, one florin, three shillings, four sixpences and five pennies. The officers also found a handkerchief, a pair of tan gloves and a card case containing some letters and a local money-lender's card. On the back of that card was a note detailing a loan of £20 made to Dickman in October 1909.

This freely made statement gave the police a great deal of new information they would not have been able to obtain from any other source, apart from Dickman himself. There was the admission that he had seen Nisbet at the station, that they had bought tickets at the

Monday, 21 March 1910

same time, that he had travelled on the same train and that he had missed his stop at Stannington and gone on to Morpeth. Whilst some of this may possibly have proved to be significant, there was little to show that Dickman was, in any way, involved in Nisbet's murder. Despite this, Dickman was then cautioned and told he would be arrested and charged with murder. In answer, Dickman replied, 'I do not understand the proceedings. It is absurd for me to deny the charge, because it is absurd to make it.'

After Dickman was charged and placed in the cells, Superintendent Weddell and other officers paid their own visit to 1 Lily Avenue and, after informing Mrs Dickman that her husband had been arrested, searched the premises. They found a batch of personal letters, two bank books, two pawn tickets, a pair of suede gloves and a pair of trousers, both apparently stained. Back at the station they also took the coat Dickman had been wearing when he was charged, a fawn coloured Burberry.

Later that evening, Dickman was transferred to the Central Police Station in Pilgrim Street, Newcastle (*see Plate 9*). It was there, that same day, that he was placed in an identity parade. Hall and Spink, the two clerks who had seen Nisbet on the train, both walked down a line of nine men. Spink was unable to pick out any man but Hall made a somewhat tentative identification of Dickman.

That evening, Dickman was sent to Newcastle Gaol in Carliol Street. It was his first night in custody for a murder which he said he had not committed (*see Plate 10*).

Chapter 6

Tuesday, 22 March to Sunday, 3 April 1910

On the day after his arrest, Tuesday, 22 March, Dickman made his first appearance before the magistrates. This was held in the charge office back at Gosforth police station.

Captain Fullerton James, the chief constable, arrived at the station at 3.45pm. Soon afterwards, the defence solicitor, Mr Edward Clark arrived to be followed by the justice of the peace, Richard Welford. Also present in the room at that time were Inspector Bousfield, the deputy clerk Mr Nicholson and a lady, seated on a chair in the centre of the room. That lady was Annie Dickman, the prisoner's wife.

Now that all the officials had taken their places, the press men were allowed in. As they filled all the vacant spaces, Annie Dickman entered a loud and vigorous protest against the taking of any photographs. When informed that photographs would not be allowed, she then demanded that no sketches should be made either, and this was seconded by Mr Clark. Mr Welford asked the gentlemen present not to make any sketches of the prisoner but Annie Dickman had still not finished. She then insisted that no sketches be made of her either.

Once all this had been agreed, John Dickman was brought into the room. He stood at the front of a desk, with his back to the press men and was formally remanded for eight days, until 30 March. As he turned to leave, he gently placed his hand on his wife's shoulder and tenderly kissed her. Annie then asked Mr Welford if her son might see his father. No objections were made.

Tuesday, 22 March to Sunday, 3 April 1910

It was also on 22 March that the funeral of the victim took place. A carriage drawn by two black horses took Nisbet's body to Jesmond Old Cemetery. Many thousands of people lined the route.

In his statement to the police, Dickman had mentioned a number of people and over the next few days they were all interviewed. To begin with, Dickman had said that he had travelled on the 10.27am train to see a Mr Hogg. When officers spoke to William Hogg he confirmed that he had known Dickman since about 1900. He had had no appointment with Dickman at Dovecot on 18 March and indeed was in Newcastle city centre all that day. However, he also went on to say that Dickman had already called on him five times about the shaft which they were sinking and on each of these occasions, no appointment had been made. His last visit had taken place two weeks earlier, on Friday, 4 March.

John Athey was the ticket collector at Morpeth station. He confirmed that on the day in question, the 10.27 from Newcastle had arrived on time. He recalled a man handing him a ticket to Stannington and an excess fare of 2.5d. The man had the ticket and the money ready in his hand and said, 'I think two and a half pence is the correct fare from Stannington.' Athey was unable to give any description of the man but said he was wearing a coat. He could not see if he carried a bag.

Dickman had also mentioned meeting a man named Elliott, whilst he was in Morpeth. In fact, he had met up with two men. The first of these was William Strafford Sanderson, a wine and spirits merchant who said that he had left his office at around 1.30pm on Friday, 18 March. As he was walking over the footbridge that led to Morpeth station he was overtaken by Edwin Elliott, who was riding a bicycle. The two men fell into conversation and as they walked, they met a man who was walking from the direction of the station. This man spoke to Elliott, and Sanderson had since been able to confirm that the man was Dickman.

At the time of the encounter, Dickman seemed perfectly normal in his demeanour. Dickman asked Elliott what he fancied for the big race, it being the day of the Grand National the next day, and Sanderson said that he had dreamed that the favourite had won. Dickman scoffed at the idea of a dream predicting the winner of a horse race.

The police seemed to think that this evidence only served to strengthen their case. Whilst it was true that both Elliott and Sanderson said that they saw no blood on Dickman's clothing, that he was not carrying a bag, and seemed to be perfectly normal in his demeanour, there was the fact that his alibi, for the time between leaving the train and his meeting with Elliott was weak, to say the least. If anything, the case was made even stronger by a development that evening.

In the evening edition of the local newspaper of 22 March there appeared a report from a gentleman named Brocklehurst. He reported that a fortnight before the murder, on 4 March, he had travelled on the 9.30am express from Newcastle to Morpeth. He was in the last compartment of the second carriage from the engine and whilst the train was somewhere between Annitsford and Stannington he heard a loud report. Upon looking out of the window he noticed that the wood outside was splintered. It appeared that someone had fired a shot out of another carriage on the train. The police, of course, seized on this to suggest that Dickman, who according to William Hogg had last visited Dovecot on 4 March, had been testing a gun to see if anyone would hear the shots. They failed to notice that of equal significance was that the shot was fired before the train reached Stannington.

Meanwhile, life for the people of Newcastle went on as normal. On Saturday, 26 March, Newcastle United played Swindon Town in the semi-final of the FA Cup. The match took place at White Hart Lane and Newcastle won 2-0.

That same day, another murder took place close to Newcastle, when Thomas Craig shot to death Thomas Henderson in Gateshead. Craig had been walking out with a young girl, Annie Finn, but he had then been sent to prison for stealing. Whilst he was serving his sentence, Annie had fallen in love with Henderson and married him.

Tuesday, 22 March to Sunday, 3 April 1910

Once he was released from prison, Craig tracked them to their new home and shot Henderson as he hung up a picture. Craig had then run from the house and disappeared into the maze of streets. The police were now engaged in a massive search for the wanted man.

On Wednesday, 30 March, Dickman was back before the magistrates. The chairman on this occasion was Mr Gerald Fenwick and as Dickman arrived in a horse-drawn cab, large crowds surged forward to catch a glimpse of him.

Superintendent Weddell gave evidence of Dickman's arrest and gave details of searches that had been made along the railway line between Stannington and Morpeth, though nothing of significance had been discovered.

Charles Raven was called to confirm that the man he had seen with Nisbet, walking through the gateway to platform 4, was the prisoner.

William Sanderson was called to confirm that Dickman had seemed perfectly normal in his behaviour when they met in Morpeth and Mr Edward Clark for the defence then asked for bail. This was refused and Dickman was remanded for a further seven days, until 6 April. The magistrate did order, however, that the money found on the prisoner at the time of his arrest should be returned to his family.

The final development during this period occurred on Sunday, 3 April. On that date, the train on which the murder had taken place was reassembled at Newcastle station and Wilson Hepple asked to take part in an experiment. He was told to take up a position outside the carriage he had travelled in on 18 March. This he easily identified as he recalled it contained a picture of Brancepeth Castle. Only one compartment had such a picture.

Once he was in position, an officer walked up the train until Hepple confirmed that he was at the position he had last seen Dickman and Nisbet together. When the officer was told to stop, he was directly outside the compartment where Nisbet's body had been found. It was yet another setback for John Alexander Dickman.

Chapter 7

Monday, 4 April to Wednesday, 13 April 1910

By this time, details where some of the passengers had been sitting on the fateful train, could be reconstructed (*see Plate 11*).

It will be seen that at the time the train left Newcastle, Andrew Bruce was in the compartment closest to the engine. This was a smoking compartment.

In the next compartment sat Percival Harding Hall and John William Spink. Their compartment was a non-smoker, as was the one Nisbet was travelling in and in which his body would later be found. Remember that according to Hall, it had been Nisbet who suggested to his companion that they should make this compartment a smoker. The companion had walked on, past Hall, who was standing looking out of the window, and along to the compartment which Bruce was travelling in.

Wilson Hepple was in the third compartment of the third carriage and the guard, Robert Wilkinson, was in the guard's van at the very end.

It is plain to see how Hall and Spink would have been able to nod to Nisbet as they waited for the train to pull out of Stannington and how Bruce would have been able to witness this. It is also clear how John Grant, who was looking for a smoking compartment, would have passed the one vacated by Hall and Spink and the one Nisbet had travelled in before choosing the first compartment of the second carriage, which was a smoker.

Seeing this layout may also go some way to explaining why no shots were heard. The murder apparently having taken place between

Monday, 4 April to Wednesday, 13 April 1910

Stannington and Morpeth, the compartment next to Nisbet's would have been empty and was also close to a noisy steam locomotive. At the time, the compartment in which Grant would sit at Morpeth might also have been empty for Grant reported that it was so, when he climbed in.

On Wednesday, 6 April, Dickman was back in court. Mr C.L. Bell presided over a bench of seven magistrates. The prisoner entered court at 11.10am, looking smart and well groomed. His wife, Annie, sat behind Dickman. It was reported that she wore a black straw hat with green wing feathers and a dark grey costume.

Mr S. Pearce appeared for the director of public prosecutions and said that the police had not yet completed their investigations and asked for a further adjournment. The defence objected to these constant remands and again asked for bail, saying that there was little evidence against the prisoner. Bail was refused but the magistrates did put some pressure on the prosecution, demanding to know if they would be ready to proceed to a conclusion, if a further remand was granted. Once they had intimated that this would almost certainly be possible, a further remand was granted, for eight days, until 11.00am, 14 April.

Returned to his cell in Newcastle gaol, John Alexander Dickman would have just eight days to wait before he saw how strong the case was against him.

Chapter 8

Thursday, 14 April to Friday, 15 April 1910

At last the evidence was to be heard. The final magistrates' court appearances took place at the Moot Hall in Newcastle (*see Plate 12*). Hundreds of people were turned away from the court, and even the yard outside. Once again, Mr C.L. Bell presided, Mr Pearce appeared for the prosecution and Mr Clark for the defence.

Mr Pearce began by reading out the basic facts of the crime and then proceeded to read out the statement Dickman had made to the police. This evidence was followed by plans of the train and photographs pertaining to the case being entered into evidence.

The first witness was Cicely Nisbet who was in court with her eldest daughter. Dressed entirely in black, Mrs Nisbet told the court of her last meeting with her husband, at Heaton station. She began,

> 'On Friday, 18th March, I went to Heaton station to meet the train. I went to the rear of the train where I usually found him. He was not there, and I thought he had missed the train, but on looking round I saw him looking out of a carriage next to the engine.'

> 'You ran along the train and your husband stood to talk to you? You had a few hurried words with him and the train went out?' asked Mr Pearce.

> 'Yes.'

'Now Mrs Nisbet, it is with extreme regret I have to ask these questions. They will be as short as possible. Did you notice whether there was another man in the compartment?'

'Yes.'

'There was another man?'

'Yes.'

'You were unable to see well, as your husband was standing by the window?'

'I could see right along the carriage, and there was a shadow on the seat.'

There was no cross examination and Mrs Nisbet made to leave the witness box. As she did so, she half fainted and had to be assisted. She was escorted from the courtroom but could be heard sobbing bitterly in the corridor outside. This would prove to be highly significant in the future.

Thomas Anderson gave details of the cheque he had handed to Nisbet on the day of the murder and John Bradshaw Wilson told how he had cashed that cheque at the bank and how the cash had been made up.

Charles Raven then gave his testimony, detailing how he had seen Nisbet and Dickman, apparently walking together towards platform 5. He agreed again that he had not seen them in conversation at any time.

Wilson Hepple then told the court how he had put some parcels in the compartment he had chosen and then stood on the platform, pacing up and down a few steps, outside the door. He said that he had seen Dickman with a man he did not know at the time, but now knew to be Nisbet. They were in conversation and walked on to the front of the train.

The next witness was Percival Harding Hall. He said he had seen Nisbet and a companion coming towards the front of the train. He could tell from their conversation that they were looking for a smoking compartment. The compartment they eventually got into was the one next to Hall's and he had heard Nisbet say they would take this one. His companion remarked that it wasn't a smoker and Nisbet replied that they would make it one. It was Nisbet who opened the door. Hall then confirmed that he had identified Dickman as the companion of Nisbet, in a line-up of nine men at the Central Police Station in Pilgrim Street.

Continuing his evidence, Hall then stated that he and Spink had left the train at Stannington. They both put their bags on the platform and waited for the train to pull out before they could cross the line and walk to the colliery at Netherton where the wages they were carrying were to be delivered. As the train pulled out he saw Nisbet and nodded to him. Nisbet returned the nod.

It was at this point, under cross examination, that there was the first inkling that Hall's identification was not all it should be. Asked to detail the words he had used when identifying Dickman, Hall replied 'I would not swear that it was the prisoner, but if I could be assured that the murderer was there, I would have no hesitation in pointing the prisoner out.'

The defence had missed an important point here. Putting aside the obvious ambiguity of the identification itself, Hall had said that he had walked down a line of nine men. Why then had he referred to the man he had picked out as 'the prisoner'? How could he know that he had picked out the man the police arrested? It could be argued that he would have assumed it if his identification had been certain but his words hardly convey that. In fact, this identification would be eventually totally discredited, but that day was far into the future.

Thursday, 14 April to Friday, 15 April 1910

John William Spink told the court that he could not identify the man in the compartment with Nisbet. He too had nodded to Nisbet at Stannington. Both Nisbet and the other man had been reading newspapers and Nisbet lowered his, but the companion kept on reading.

Andrew Bruce confirmed that he had travelled in the first compartment and had seen Hall and Spink nod to someone on the train. John Grant then confirmed that the murder compartment appeared to be empty at Morpeth and John Thomas Cosher, the porter at Longhirst said the same. He had walked down the train, from the engine to the rear, and had seen that the compartment in question was empty.

Thomas William Charlton, the porter at Alnmouth, told of his finding of the body and John Athey, the ticket collector at Morpeth, was called to try to identify the prisoner as the man who had given him the ticket for Stannington and an excess fare. He was asked if Dickman was the man and said that he was. This was hardly startling evidence since Dickman freely admitted that he had alighted at Morpeth and paid the extra fare from Stannington. Further, it did not explain why Dickman was not seen leaving the carriage where the crime was committed.

Detective Inspector Tait told of his visit to Dickman's home and the subsequent statement made by the prisoner. That statement was entered into evidence by the next witness, Superintendent Weddell, who read it to the court. Some letters from Annie Dickman to her husband were also entered into evidence, in some of which she had referred to being short of money and not knowing how to pay the bills, thus apparently confirming their financial concerns.

After Constable Nisbet, the first officer on the scene, had given his evidence, the prosecution called Henrietta Hymen who ran a newsagent's shop from premises at 35 Groat Market. She allowed people to have mail delivered there and one man who took advantage of this service was John Dickman, though he had first told her that his surname was Black. She referred to a parcel, which by the shape she determined to be a revolver. This had been sent to Mr Black but was followed by a postcard from a gun dealer, saying that it had been sent in error. When he picked it up, Mr Black asked for a label to return it. Matters were then adjourned to the following day.

On Friday, 15 April, a dreary, rainy morning, the first witness was William Hogg who repeated what he had told the police about knowing Dickman for some ten years and having no appointment to see him on 18 March. He was followed by Dr Charles Clarke Burnham who detailed the wounds Nisbet had suffered.

The next witness was Andrew Craig Kirkwood, a gentleman who worked for Messrs Pape and Co, gunsmiths. He showed the court that there was an entry in his register of sales showing that a 'John A. Dickinson' of Lily Avenue had purchased an automatic pistol in 1907.

Thomas Simpson, who worked for the same gunsmiths, gave details of the four bullets that had been found. He confirmed that the two nickel-plated .250 bullets could have been fired by the automatic pistol Kirkwood had referred to. Asked if the assailant must have had two weapons, Simpson replied, 'Certainly.'

The prosecution case closed and Mr Clark then summed up for the defence. He claimed there was nothing in the way of evidence to connect his client with the crime. After a long and impassioned speech, the magistrates retired for half an hour and then returned to court and announced that in their opinion a prima-facie case had been made against the prisoner. He would be remanded once more, to Thursday, 21 April, when the depositions would be read over. He would then be sent for trial at the next assizes, which were due to be held in June.

John Dickman might have thought that the worst of his ordeal before the magistrates was over. He could not have been more wrong.

Chapter 9

Saturday, 16 April to Wednesday, 8 June 1910

The next few days saw another event finally take Dickman's name out of the newspapers. On Saturday, 16 April, Thomas Craig, the man who had shot dead Thomas Henderson in Gateshead, on 26 March, was finally captured by the police, in Dilston. This filled a good few pages but soon, it was Dickman who was back in the headlines.

On 21 April, Dickman made his final appearance before the magistrates. It should merely have been a formality but it was to prove to be anything but.

Dickman entered the court, looked around and smiled at his wife. At that point, Cicely Nisbet was assisted into the witness box and, after her deposition had been read over to her, she asked if she might make a statement. Given permission, she then said that the reason she had fainted on the day she gave her evidence at the magistrates' court was because as she left the witness box, she had caught a glimpse of the prisoner in profile. She had immediately recognised it as being identical to the profile she had seen in the railway compartment with her husband on the day he was killed. As a result, she was now absolutely certain that the man in that compartment was none other than John Alexander Dickman. It was yet more evidence against Dickman who was later formally sent for trial.

For the time being, Newcastle found other pastimes to attract the attention of its citizens. On Saturday, 23 April, Newcastle United played Barnsley in the final of the FA Cup, at Crystal Palace. The match was a 1-1 draw but at the replay, at Goodison Park on Thursday, 28 April, Newcastle ran out winners, 2-0. It was the first time the team had ever won the coveted trophy. That same day, 28 April, the adjourned inquest on Nisbet reopened and formally returned a verdict of wilful murder against Dickman.

On 21 May, the dead man's widow, Cicely Nisbet, had her 40th birthday, though it is likely she did not celebrate it under the circumstances.

The public at large, the police who had investigated the case, and all those involved in it, no doubt believed that nothing new could come to light until the trial itself. They could not know that an event in early June would prove them to be totally wrong.

Chapter 10

Thursday, 9 June 1910

There had been problems with the Isabella mine shaft at the Hepscott colliery. In February, 1910, the shaft had been used to bring up some of the mineworkers by sling as the main shaft, some 200 yards away, was temporarily out of order. After that, the Isabella had not been used, as it was liable to flooding. It was still, however, subject to regular inspections.

Peter Spooner had examined the bottom of the shaft on Thursday, 17 March, the day before Nisbet had been killed. He had subsequently examined it again on Friday, 29 April and Wednesday, 18 May. On both of these occasions he had noticed nothing out of the ordinary. Now, on Thursday, 9 June, it was time to inspect the shaft again.

Spooner finished his inspection and was turning to go back the way he had come when he saw a bundle lying on the ground, partly buried in the mud and clay. He picked the object up and found that it was a large leather wallet and shaking it, he heard what sounded like the jangling of coins. Searching around the bottom of the shaft he found other coins, all of them copper. It was obvious that he had found the missing wages bag. Spooner wasted no time in taking the bag up out of the mine and contacting the police.

There could be no doubt that the bag found was the one that Nisbet had been carrying on the day he had been murdered, for the colliery pay slips, still inside, confirmed it. Perhaps the statement made by Spooner will best sum up the event.

> On the 9th June I was inspecting the two shafts. I held
> my lamp up to look up the shaft. I saw something lying,

which looked like a Navvies smock. We find all such things down the shaft – dead dogs etc.

I walked away six or seven paces and the thought struck me that I would have a look at the thing. I then turned and put my stick on it and turned it over and saw it was a bag.

The bag was lying top down and partly covered by clay, which falls off the shaft sides. The bag was lying in a depression, or hole at the side of the shaft bottom and was wedged in tight and was very bad to see from the old shaft bottom.

I was previously there on the 18th May and previously to that on 29th April and on 17th March.

My duty is to see that the shaft is clear, but I do not necessarily look at the bottom. It is quite dark where the bag was lying and unless I had turned the lamp on to it I should not have seen it even then.

The bag was examined by the police, who found a large tear down one side. The lock was damaged and it seemed clear that the thief had tried to force it open and, having failed, had then taken a knife and slashed at the leather in order to remove the contents.

A further search of the bottom of the shaft was made by the police, and more coins were discovered. Spooner himself had recovered the sum of 14s 6d and the police search discovered a further 4s 9d. In all, that made a total of 19s 3d, all in copper coinage. It should be remembered that originally the bag had held £1 0s 6d in copper, which the bank cashier had wrapped in a small brown paper parcel. Now, only 1s 3d of that copper remained unaccounted for. It seemed clear that whoever had taken that bag from Nisbet, had only taken the gold and the silver and thrown the rest down the mineshaft. There was, however, a major problem for the police to overcome (*see Plate 13*).

Thursday, 9 June 1910

John Alexander Dickman had been in custody since Monday, 21 March. If he was the killer then he had only three days in which to dispose of the incriminating bank bag and, most likely, would have done so on the day of the murder, Friday, 18 March. That meant that the bag had been lying at the bottom of the shaft during two previous inspections and Spooner had missed it. That of course was entirely possible. After all, the shaft was very dark, but it must be remembered that Spooner had a lamp with him on every occasion. The possibility that someone had dropped the bag down the shaft at a later date was simply ignored. It didn't fit the scenario of Dickman being the killer, and therefore it just couldn't have happened. They also missed another important point.

Assuming Dickman was the killer, he would most likely have dumped the bank bag on the day of the murder. We then have to assume that he either dumped the gun or guns he had used in a different location or kept them with him. Keeping them with him does not make sense as he might well have been stopped at any time. He could not have known that the body would not be discovered until after noon. Dumping them in a different location also does not make sense. The mineshaft was the perfect place. Logic dictates that someone else might well be the killer and had dumped the bag after 18 March, to deliberately incriminate a man already in custody. That possibility too was not even considered.

When Spooner was questioned by the police he admitted that he did know Dickman, and they had even once worked together for the same mining company. They had met occasionally since and Spooner had talked about mining, that colliery in particular and the fact that it was liable to flooding. He had to also admit, though, that as far as he knew, Dickman did not know where the Isabella shaft actually was.

There was something else that Dickman would not have known, though again that was ignored by the police. It had been some considerable time since Spooner and Dickman had spoken and the Isabella shaft had only been closed a few weeks before the murder.

How then would Dickman have known that the shaft was now out of use?

The facts had to be fitted to the assumption that Dickman was guilty. In order to explain this we need to refer back to the map of the area, shown in this chapter.

Dickman said he had missed his stop at Stannington, got out at Morpeth and, walking to the west, had walked towards the Dovecot colliery. That meant he would have taken the road to the left of the railway line. He said that halfway along the route he fell ill and had to take a rest in a field. It took some time for his illness to pass and he then decided to walk back to Morpeth instead. The spot where he climbed into a field to rest is shown, approximately, by the X on the map.

According to the police version of events, Dickman was lying. He had indeed left Morpeth station but he had turned instead to the east and had walked down the road to the right of the railway line, towards the Isabella shaft. Somewhere along that road, probably at the shaft itself, he had slashed open the bag and removed the gold and silver. He had then dropped the bag down the shaft before returning to Morpeth where he met up with Elliott and Sanderson, before catching the 1.40pm slow train back to Newcastle.

The finding of the bag was the last event in the case before the trial itself. All Dickman could do now was wait for his day in court.

Chapter 11

Friday, 10 June to Sunday, 3 July 1910

It was again a time of quiet before the trial. The date had now been set. Dickman's trial would start on 4 July and was expected to last two or three days. Counsel had been determined. The trial judge had been appointed for the assizes. All was ready. Dickman waited, languishing in his cell, knowing that public opinion was set strongly against him.

Even now, mistakes were made. At this stage, Dickman's name was cursed in the city of Newcastle, yet the trial was to take place in this hostile city. Readers will recall the mention of Thomas Craig who had shot a man dead in Gateshead. There could be little doubt that he would be found guilty, for his name was also cursed in the Newcastle area. It was for that reason that Craig's defence team sought and won the right for him to be tried at Durham. There was little chance of saving him, but at least he would get a fair hearing, away from the location of his murder.

In fact, Craig's trial took place on Saturday, 25 June, before Mr Justice Grantham. Craig's defence was that the killing of Thomas William Henderson was an accident. He admitted that he had shot him but only intended to wound him. There was also the fact that he had suffered extreme provocation due to the fact that he had lost the only woman he had ever loved.

The jury retired to consider their verdict. When it came, it was that Craig was guilty of murder but they wished to add a recommendation to mercy. Craig was duly sentenced to death but at least his team had tried everything to save him.

The same could not be said for Dickman. He would face a jury in the home town of the man he was accused of killing, where public opinion was extremely hostile.

Chapter 12

Monday, 4 July 1910 – Early Witnesses

The trial of John Alexander Dickman opened at the Moot Hall, Newcastle on Monday, 4 July 1910, before Lord Coleridge. The case for the prosecution was led by Mr Edward Tindal Atkinson, assisted by Mr Charles Frederick Lowenthal. The prisoner was defended by Mr Edward Alfred Mitchell-Innes who was assisted by Lord William Percy (*see Plate 14*).

A large crowd, estimated at between 1,000 and 1,500 people had gathered in the area around the court, hoping to catch a glimpse of the prisoner, as he arrived in the prison van. Some of the crowd were positioned there a good two hours before the proceedings were due to open at 11.00am. Dickman's wife, Annie, who would not be called to give evidence, occupied a seat in the public gallery.

The trial opened with a long speech from Mr Tindal Atkinson for the prosecution, during which he outlined the facts of the case. In that speech he agreed that the case consisted entirely of circumstantial evidence and then went on to describe Nisbet, the mild-mannered, slightly built victim of the crime who had only stood five feet four inches in height.

Mr Atkinson went on to outline the testimony that would be given by the four main witnesses all of whom, in one form or another, had identified Dickman as the man seen with Nisbet on the day in question. These four were Charles Raven, Wilson Hepple, Percival Harding Hall and Cicely Nisbet.

When referring to the train pulling into Morpeth, counsel appeared to contradict himself. First he confirmed that the murder carriage appeared to be empty there, but then went on to say that Dickman, by his own admission, had alighted from the train at that station. The implication was that Dickman must have left the 'empty' murder compartment without being seen, although as we will see, John Grant said that he was on the platform, next to where the carriage stopped, and it was empty when the train pulled in.

The matter of the weapons was then discussed and Mr Atkinson confirmed that it was his opinion that two weapons must have been used. He then moved on to Dickman's interview with the police, the statement he had made and his subsequent arrest, before discussing the finding of the bank bag in a shaft some one and three quarter miles south of Morpeth station. Finally he referred to certain items of forensic evidence and to Dickman's apparent financial predicaments at the time the crime was committed. The trial proper could then begin.

The first few witnesses merely produced documents that would be needed for the case. Thus Walter Henry Dickenson produced a plan of part of Newcastle Central station and a railway timetable. He also confirmed that the train in question arrived at Morpeth at 11.12am, and was due to wait there for four minutes whilst it took on water. Dickenson also stated that there was a slow train back to Newcastle, which left Morpeth at 11.24am, an express from Morpeth to Newcastle at 1.12pm and a further slow train at 1.40pm.

Dickenson was followed to the witness stand by Mark Watson Ramsay, who produced four photographs, which he had taken of the gateway to the platforms and the train. There followed a brief interlude during which Mr Atkinson drew the judge's attention to the rather stifling atmosphere in the court. The judge replied that he had already spoken to the authorities on the matter but there was little they could do to provide extra ventilation.

The next witness was Charles Franklin Murphy, a surveyor, who had prepared a plan of the district around Morpeth and Stannington. He was also able to confirm that the Isabella shaft was one and three

Monday, 4 July 1910 – Early Witnesses

quarter miles from Morpeth and the distance from Stannington station to the Dovecot colliery was one and three eighths miles and finally, from Morpeth to Dovecot was three and three quarter miles.

Thomas Anderson, then told the court that on 18 March, he had handed Nisbet a cheque for the colliery wages. He confirmed that Nisbet made this same journey every alternate Friday and thus had previously made the trip on 4 March. The money would always be placed into a lockable black leather bag, which was some nine inches in length. He had seen the bag recovered from the pit-shaft and confirmed that it was the one Nisbet had used.

John Bradshaw Wilson then took the stand and confirmed that he had cashed the cheque in question. The gold was in three canvas bags, the silver in paper bags and the copper in a brown paper parcel. There followed some discussion about what type of canvas bags had been used. When Dickman had been searched at the police station, some of the gold he carried was in a Lambton's Bank canvas bag. Wilson worked for Lloyds Bank but Lambton's had amalgamated with Lloyds and his bank now used both types. The inference was that the bag found in Dickman's possession had come from the ones handed over by Wilson, but Mr Mitchell-Innes was able to mention that Dickman had had an account at Lambton's for some years.

These early witnesses had done nothing to incriminate Dickman, but four of the next five would add greatly to the weight of prosecution evidence.

Chapter 13

Monday, 4 July 1910 – Identifications

The first of the witnesses called to identify Dickman as the man seen with Nisbet, was Charles Raven.

Raven began by confirming that he had known Nisbet to speak to for five or six years, but had not known him by name. At about 10.20am, he was at the Central station and approached the gateway to platform 4 from the west side of the station. The first-class and third-class tea rooms were on his left, and there were not many people about. When he was some three yards from the gate he saw Nisbet walking with the prisoner. They were walking together and passed through the gate to the platform. He saw them turn to the right, behind a cigar shop, and head off towards platform 5. They were not in conversation.

The next witness was the artist, Wilson Hepple. He confirmed that he had known Dickman for some twenty years. On 18 March, he was in the Central station and saw Dickman in the ticket hall. Hepple said that he was the second person at the ticket window and saw Dickman, further down the queue, as he left the ticket hall.

After purchasing his ticket, Hepple walked to platform 5 and selected his compartment on the train. He had some parcels with him and placed these inside the compartment but stayed out on the platform for a few minutes. He then paced up and down, outside the carriage door, taking three or four steps in each direction. Whilst he was walking up and down Hepple saw Dickman with a companion, who he did not notice particularly, apart from the fact that he was of slight build. He believed that they were in conversation, as their faces were turned towards each other.

Monday, 4 July 1910 – Identifications

At one stage, Hepple's walk took him in the direction of the engine and he noticed that Dickman and his companion were about to board the train. One of them had his hand on the handle of the compartment door as Hepple turned back to walk the other way. By the time he turned back, the two men had disappeared.

Under cross examination, Hepple stated that he had been walking up and down for some considerable time before he saw Dickman and his companion and that the time elapsing between his last sighting of them and the train pulling out of the station would have been about one minute.

Hepple was asked further questions about the timings for that day. He said that he had arrived at the station at about 10.07am. The booking office window was not open at that time. Hepple then walked to the main platform until the railway officials put a board up showing that the train was to depart from platform 5. This was after quite a considerable time. Hepple immediately returned to the booking office and purchased his ticket, being the second customer in the line. It was then that he noticed Dickman in the hall. Asked to determine how long he had been pacing up and down, Hepple answered that it was perhaps seven or eight minutes.

The final questions related to the distance Dickman had been from Hepple on the platform. It was then confirmed that the platform was some eighteen feet wide and that Dickman and his companion had been that far away when Hepple had seen them.

Before moving on to the evidence of the next witness, a point should be made about the very basics of Hepple's evidence. The train in question had, of course, left from platform 5 at 10.27am. Two local newspapers, *The Evening Chronicle* and the *Illustrated Chronicle* state that in Hepple's testimony he referred to catching the 10.29am train. That may have been a simple typographical error but we will refer back to this point in a later chapter.

Percival Harding Hall then took the stand. He confirmed that he had known Nisbet as the Widdrington cashier for some four or five years.

Hall had been performing the same duty of carrying wages for that period but said he had never travelled in the same compartment as Nisbet.

Hall went on to say that on 18 March, he had travelled on the 10.27am in the company of Spink. They had got into the second compartment of the first coach and Spink sat down on the seat. Hall, however, went to the window and looked out. As he did so he saw Nisbet and another man coming towards him. When he first saw them they were eight or ten yards away. It was Nisbet who opened the door of the compartment next to Hall's and the two men got in very close to the time the train departed.

At Stannington station, he and Spink had left the train. They had to wait for the train to pull out before they could cross the line and continue on foot to Netherton colliery with the workmen's wages. As the train begin to leave, Hall saw Nisbet and bowed to him but could not tell if there was anyone in the compartment with him.

Having heard of the murder, Hall went to the police and gave a description of the man he had seen with Nisbet at Newcastle. He then referred to the identification parade and confirmed his rather ambiguous comments regarding his selection of Dickman. It was on this matter that Hall was given an extremely rough time by the defence barrister, Mr Mitchell-Innes.

The defence barrister began,

> I want to ask you a question about the so-called identification. You went down to the police station I understand?

Hall simply answered,

> 'Yes.'

> 'There you found the policeman. Who was the policeman you first saw there?'

Monday, 4 July 1910 – Identifications

'I saw a number together.'

'Can you mention one who seemed to be in control, who took you into the room or place where these men were? What was his name?'

'I could not say who it was.'

'Do you know Superintendent Weddell?'

'I know Superintendent Weddell.'

'Was he there?'

'I think he was there. He was there later anyhow.'

Having failed to determine precisely which officer took charge of the identification parade, Mr Mitchell-Innes turned to the process itself.

'You went into the room and you found nine men standing in a row?'

'Quite so.'

'I put it to you that you walked more than once; two or three times up and down the row and picked out nobody?'

'I walked once down the row.'

'I put it to you that you walked more than once.'

'I think not.'

'You think not. Will you swear that you did not walk more than once? Be careful.'

Hall hesitated a long time before replying. He had to be prompted to do so before saying that to the best of his knowledge he had only walked down the line once, looking at each man. Pressed further on the matter, Hall finally said that he could not swear that he did not walk down the line more than once.

Mr Mitchell-Innes continued,

> 'I put it to you that you then went away from the row of men and approached the officer, Is that right?'
>
> 'That is so.'
>
> 'And you said to that officer something. What was it?'
>
> 'I asked him what I was expected to do.'
>
> 'By that time you had already walked down the line at least once?'
>
> 'At least once.'
>
> 'Do you mean to say that you had not been told before you walked down the line what you were expected to do? What had you gone there for?'
>
> 'I had gone to try and identify the companion of Nisbet.'
>
> 'Why did you ask the policeman what you were to do?'
>
> 'Because I wanted to know if, by pointing out a certain man, I was swearing that this was the man I saw get in with Nisbet.'

Hall was then questioned about the idea that he would be swearing to an identification. He had, after all, not taken any oath. His reply was that is what he believed making an identification meant.

Mr Mitchell-Innes returned to the reply the officer had made when Hall asked him what he was supposed to do. Hall replied that the policeman had said, 'Point him out.'

Monday, 4 July 1910 – Identifications

The cross-examination now turned to the words used when Hall had made his identification of Dickman. Mr Mitchell-Innes began, 'What did you say in answer to his direction?'

'I said that I would not swear that the man I was going to point out was the companion of Nisbet, but that if I was assured that the murderer was there, I would have no hesitation in pointing out that man, and I pointed to the prisoner.'

This phraseology was slightly different to what Hall had said at the magistrates' court and further questions now tried to clear up the actual words Hall had used. Eventually Mr Mitchell-Innes summarised the matter for Hall saying, 'Your account today, whether it differs from the account before the magistrates, is that you walked, you will not swear whether it was more than once, down the line, and then you asked a police constable what you should do. He told you to point him out. Will you just tell us the rest?' Hall reiterated what he had said before, adding that they were the effect of his words but what he actually said might have been slightly different. Mr Mitchell-Innes had one final point to make.

'Did you use the word murderer because you had formed some conclusion in your mind with regard to this case?'

'No, not at all.'

'It was simply a pleasant way of referring to the prisoner?'

There was no reply to that question and it was a much relieved Hall who finally stepped down from the witness box.

Hall was followed by his fellow clerk, John William Spink. He had seen nothing of Nisbet or a companion at Newcastle so his testimony really began with him leaving the train at Stannington. He confirmed that he and Hall had put their bags on the platform whilst they waited for the train to leave. It was then that he saw Nisbet in the next compartment, with a companion. Nisbet was at the far side of the compartment, facing the engine. His companion sat directly opposite to him. He had seen the two men before the train began to pull out. All Spink could say about the companion was that he wore a black felt hat, and had a moustache. He had been unable to identify Dickman as that man.

The final identification witness was Cicely Elizabeth Nisbet. She began by detailing her habit of meeting her husband's train at Heaton on the Fridays when he was due to take the wages up to Widdrington.

Nisbet usually travelled at the back of the train but on this particular day he wasn't there and, looking up she saw him look out of a carriage window close to the engine. She ran along the platform and had time to have a brief conversation with him, during which she noticed a man in the same compartment. He was sitting facing the engine at the far end of the compartment. She only saw his profile and he had his hat pulled down and his collar pulled up.

Cicely then spoke of the magistrates' hearing where, after giving her evidence, she had fainted. This was because she had seen his profile again in the same position and was now quite certain that the man in the dock was the one who had travelled with her husband.

It was during his cross examination that Mr Mitchell-Innes made one of his worst mistakes of the trial. He pressed Cicely on the certainty of her identification. At the magistrates' court she had only said that Dickman resembled strongly the man she had seen in profile but now she was absolutely certain. Unfortunately, when questioning her, the defence barrister referred to her throughout as Mrs Dickman, until Cicely remonstrated with him and asked him to correct himself. Whatever seeds of doubt he might have placed in the minds of the jury had been destroyed by that unthinking mistake.

The damage had been done. Despite his attempts to cast doubts on the evidence of identification, four witnesses had firmly placed Dickman with Nisbet on the day the latter had been killed.

Chapter 14

Monday, 4 July 1910 – Later Witnesses

The next witness was John Athey, the ticket collector at Morpeth. He confirmed that a man had handed him a Stannington ticket and an excess fare. He was unable to positively identify Dickman as the man who had done this but, of course, that was irrelevant. Dickman had freely admitted that he had.

John Grant told of his joining the train at Morpeth and noting that the compartment in which Nisbet's body was later found, appeared to be empty. Grant was adamant that had there been anyone sitting in there, he would have seen him. He also confirmed that he had seen Andrew Bruce in the first compartment, sitting at the platform side, with his back to the engine.

John Thomas Cosher was a porter at Longhirst station. As the train pulled in, he was close to the engine end. He saw the last witness, John Grant, leave the train but saw no one in the compartment where the murder had taken place (*see Plate 15*).

George Harker was the stationmaster at Pegswood. His evidence added nothing to the case beyond saying that he saw two passengers alight: a woman and a little girl (*see Plate 16*).

George Yeoman was the stationmaster at Longhirst. He saw three people leave the train, one of whom was John Grant. He also stated that he knew Nisbet well and often used to speak to him when the train passed through, but he did not see him on the train on 18 March.

Andrew Bruce confirmed his journey on the fateful train and to seeing Hall and Spink alight at Stannington and put their bags down on the platform as they waited for the train to leave. He saw the shorter of the two men nod to someone on the train, just as it started to move. He now knew that the shorter man was Hall, so it was he who nodded.

Thomas William Charlton repeated the details of his finding of the body. He was followed by Robert Wilkinson, the guard, who stated that he had been present at Newcastle on 3 April, when the murder train was reconstructed at the station.

Matters now turned to Dickman's financial concerns, and to the police investigation itself. William Hogg took the stand and confirmed that he had known Dickman for between eight and ten years. Hogg ran the operations at the Dovecot mine and had no appointment to see Dickman on 18 March. Dickman had, however, visited him before, the last occasion being on 4 March, but he did not have an appointment on that date either. He arrived around noon and, assumed that it would take around half an hour to walk from Stannington station. On 4 March, he had given Dickman a lift to Morpeth after his visit was concluded.

Hogg was also able to say that Dickman had once asked him for money. That had been around December 1909 when Dickman had asked for a loan of £2, saying he was in need of a couple of sovereigns to tide him over. Hogg had given him a sovereign.

It was time for the police to give their evidence and the first officer on the stand was Detective Inspector Andrew Tait of the Newcastle city police. He told of his visit to Dickman's house and the details of Dickman's subsequent arrest. Evidence of the state of Dickman's finances was then given.

When Dickman had been arrested a money-lender's card had been found upon his person. This card bore a memo, showing that Dickman had taken out a £20 loan from a company named Cash Accommodation and Investment, which was run by Samuel Cohen from premises at 130 Northumberland Street in Newcastle. The loan had been taken out in October 1909.

Monday, 4 July 1910 – Later Witnesses

Tait was followed to the witness box by Superintendent John Weddell, who was stationed at Gosforth. After giving details of Dickman's arrest, he also turned to the matter of Dickman's finances.

Weddell referred to finding two pawn tickets. One was dated 1 March from J.E. Wilson of 12 Pilgrim Street and referred to a pair of field glasses or binoculars. The name John Wilkinson was given by Dickman and an address at 180 Westmoreland Road. The amount raised had been 12s 1d.

The second pawn ticket, also for a pair of field glasses, was made the day before Nisbet's murder, 17 March, at James Somerfield and Sons of Pink Lane. Once again, the name John Wilkinson had been used. Weddell then referred to other articles he had taken possession of, including bank books and clothing. Other witnesses would later detail the significance of these items.

There followed a reference to the medical evidence. The witness, Dr Charles Clarke Burnham did little to clarify matters, changing the original order of the wounds he had listed at the magistrates' court. In effect, he gave details of five wounds, which he had found in Nisbet's head.

The first wound was directly under the left eye. It was a large wound and the bullet which had caused it had passed underneath the nose, through the bones and had punctured the right cheek bone. It was a lead bullet and was found in the temple bone on the right side of the face.

The second wound was on the left side of the forehead, over the left eyebrow. It was a superficial wound and had been caused by a nickel-plated bullet, which had been found in the wound. The wound showed little sign of burning, indicating that the weapon used was not held close to the face. The direction of the wound was downwards.

The third wound was a puncture wound behind the right ear. The bullet had only just penetrated the tissues of the skin and had not penetrated the bone. The path of the wound was straight inwards.

The fourth wound was behind the left ear. Again it was a fairly superficial wound and only slight injury had been caused to the bones beneath.

The fifth and final wound was also below the left ear and two inches lower than the fourth one. This was a large, ragged wound and the bullet had entered the skull, penetrated the cerebellum and the medulla and had come to rest behind the right eye. This too was a lead bullet. The wound direction was upwards, across the face and had cut through Nisbet's overcoat collar meaning that the collar must have been up when the gun was fired.

At that point, the court was adjourned. There would be new witnesses on the second day.

Chapter 15

Tuesday, 5 July 1910 – The Final Witnesses

The second day opened with the recall of John Athey, the ticket collector from Morpeth station. He was now asked if he could swear to the colour of the overcoat that the man who paid the excess fare was wearing. He was unable to do so. Further questioned he added that he could not say if the man carried a bag of any kind, because he did not see his right hand.

Matters then moved on to the subject of firearms. Henrietta Hymen, testified that she ran a newsagent's and stationer's from 35 Groat Market and as part of that business, allowed people to use it as an accommodation address. The prisoner had letters addressed to her shop, but in the name of Fred Black. He did not inform her of his real name until January 1910.

In October 1909, Black told her that he was expecting a gun to be delivered and, shortly afterwards, a long parcel arrived. A few weeks later a postcard arrived, from Bell Brothers of Waterloo Road, Glasgow, asking for the return of the revolver as it had been sent in error. Soon afterwards another, smaller parcel arrived. Asked what kind of letters Mr Black used to receive, Henrietta said that most of them were referring to betting matters.

The next person to take the stand was Thomas Simpson from Pape and Co, gunsmiths of Collingwood Street. He referred to the four bullets, which had been recovered from the murder scene and Nisbet's body. Two were .250 nickel-plated and two were .320 and leaden. The smaller bullets would have been fired from an automatic pistol, which would contain seven bullets when fully loaded. The larger, lead bullets could not have been fired from the same gun.

Andrew Craig Kirkwood also worked for Papes and produced the register of firearms that the firm was legally obliged to keep. There was an entry, in his handwriting but, since there could be no certainty over who had actually sold the gun in question, the register was not admitted as evidence.

The prosecution now turned to forensic matters relating to some of Dickman's clothing. Dr Robert Boland had examined a pair of suede gloves, a pair of trousers and a fawn-coloured Burberry overcoat.

On the palm of the left glove he had found a stain some three quarters of an inch by a quarter of an inch. He had tested the stain and it proved to be blood but Dr Boland was unable to say if it was human or animal.

There were nine small stains inside the front left pocket of the trousers, well down inside the pocket. The largest of these stains was about the size of a large pinhead. These too were blood.

Turning to the Burberry coat, Dr Boland said there was a large stain on the front, at the left. The surface of the material was frayed as if it had been rubbed hard and it smelled faintly of paraffin. There was no trace of blood on the coat but Dr Boland stated that if there had been blood present, the paraffin would have masked his tests and removed all detectable traces.

Peter Spooner was the next witness and he told of his finding of the bank bag in June. Superintendent Thomas Marshall of the Morpeth police then testified that he had received the bag from Spooner, and had made his own search of the shaft the following day.

Financial matters were then returned to. Robert Sweeney said he had known Dickman for five or six years. The last time he had seen him was around October 1909, when Dickman had called at his office and asked to borrow £10. He did not say why he wanted the money.

Samuel Cohen, the owner of the Cash Accommodation and Investment Company who traded from offices in Northumberland

Tuesday, 5 July 1910 – The Final Witnesses

Street referred to Dickman calling at his premises on 15 October 1909, asking for a loan of £20 which he would need for about three months. Cohen told him that the interest would be £1 per month. Dickman said he would consider the matter and left.

On 18 October, Dickman returned and said he would take the loan. He signed a promissory note for the amount of £20. The interest was correctly paid each month. After three months, or sometime around January 1910, Dickman returned and said he could not repay the principle and asked to extend the loan for a further three months. Cohen agreed to this and the final payment of interest was made on 17 March.

In November 1909, Dickman had written to Cohen enquiring about the possibility of a loan of £200, required by a gentleman named Christie. Dickman later introduced this man to Cohen and the larger loan was agreed. Details of this loan would later be given in court, by Christie himself.

The final part of Cohen's testimony, under cross examination, showed that the loan of £20 had since been repaid in full. Mrs Dickman had come into the office and paid it on 9 May.

A Mr Kettering, a partner in a jewellers in Collingwood Street, stated that Dickman had come into his shop on 14 February and pledged a pair of gold collar studs and some sleeve-links for £5. Dickman had said that he needed the £5 to go to Liverpool. Those items had not been redeemed and Kettering still held them.

John Dennis Badcock was a cashier at the National Provincial Bank in Moseley Street. Dickman had held an account there and Badcock produced copies of the transactions since December 1907, up until the last one on 29 November 1909.

On 30 June 1909, the credit balance was just 7d. Since that time, there had been three credits: one for £4 10s, one for £20 and one for £200. The latter two credits were cheques drawn by Samuel Cohen, the first payable to Dickman himself and the second payable to F. Christie and correctly countersigned by him so that it could be paid into Dickman's account. Various withdrawals had been made until, by 31 December, the account was overdrawn by 3s.

Robert Sedcole was a clerk at Lloyds Bank and Dickman had held an account there too. The last payment in had been on 13 May 1909, which was the sum of £10. There had been various withdrawals and charges since then so that now the balance was nil.

Thomas Paisley was the treasurer of the Co-Operative Society at 103 Newgate Street and that was where Annie Dickman held her account. On 30 October 1907, there was a credit balance of £73 17s 2d. There were three dividend payments in after that time, but also a large number of withdrawals. The balance now was just £4.

Frank Christie was a coal merchant and he had known Dickman for about six years. Christie had often placed bets with Dickman and it was at his suggestion that he arranged to borrow £200 from Mr Cohen. The cheque was signed over to Dickman who paid it into his account. Eventually, Christie used about half of the money for his own purposes, but the rest he had placed bets with, not very successfully.

More financial testimony was given by William Albert Christie, who was no relation to the last witness. He was a clerk in the Savings Bank of the Post Office. He produced copies of Annie Dickman's account which showed that though there had been a good deal of money paid into the account over the years, the balance now stood at just 10s 9d.

The final witness was James Irving, an acting inspector of police, based at Gosforth. He had been in charge of Dickman at the police court on 14 April. At one stage, Dickman tried to explain away the pawning of items by saying,

> There is nothing in that evidence about the pawn tickets. When racing you get mixed up with the Bigg Market boys, and after the season is over they are always asking you for money. One pair of the field glasses were my

Tuesday, 5 July 1910 – The Final Witnesses

own, the other I got from a friend who owed me some money. I took them and pawned them myself, so that if any of the boys asked me for money I could pull out the pawn tickets and say 'Look here, this is what I am down to' and they think you are hard up.

The case for the prosecution had closed. It was time for the defence to call their witnesses, but there would only be one. It was time for John Alexander Dickman to take the stand.

Chapter 16

Tuesday, 5 July 1910 – Dickman's Evidence

The evidence of John Dickman deserves to be quoted in detail. He was questioned by Lord Percy for the defence, and the summary of his evidence is given here.

I am a married man, with a son and a daughter, and have lived in Newcastle all my life. At present I live at 1 Lily Avenue, Jesmond. I have lived at different places, but always in the neighbourhood.

In 1903 I was secretary to a syndicate which was formed to purchase the Morpeth Colliery Company. The colliery was at Morpeth, it was the Howburn Colliery. When I was secretary I negotiated the sale to Messrs Moore, Brown and Fletcher, through Mr Frank Christie, in the year 1905 or 1906. I think I drew £500 or £550 commission.

Between the years 1903 and 1906 I had a legacy left to me. It consisted of some shares in the Wiltshire and Dorsetshire Bank, amounting to about £220.

After leaving the employment of the colliery I took a holiday, and also occupied my time by racing occasionally, when it suited me. I put considerable sums of money on races, sometimes as much as £100, £50 or £30. I have put money on horses for a witness in the case named Christie.

At that time I kept on the old colliery office, but I gave it up when the owners altered the building. It was in the

Tuesday, 5 July 1910 – Dickman's Evidence

Exchange Buildings. I gave it up about the end of the year 1907 or 1908. I was always very fortunate, but I have had bad periods, like most betting men.

I know the witness Cohen. He is a money lender. I introduced Mr Frank Christie to him last November. As a result of that Mr Cohen lent Christie £200. I retained £150 of this sum. It was for betting transactions but was not very successful and lost, I should think, about £110 or so.

I know Mr Hogg very well, intimately in fact. They are sinking a new shaft at the Dovecot colliery. Mr Hogg has stated that they started driving that shaft in October last.

In the early part of this year I went on several occasions to see Mr Hogg at Stannington. I did not go there in connection with these sinking operations entirely. I went to see him in regard to a private transaction with Mr Christie.

The last time that I went to see Mr Hogg before the 18th of March was a fortnight previously. It was never my custom, when I went to see Mr Hogg to make an appointment with him. He was always glad to see me, and I to see him.

On the 18th March, it was probably ten o'clock when I left my house. I was wearing the same clothes I have on now, except for the trousers. When I left my home I took a tram, which stops at Fern Avenue. I got off at the foot of Northumberland Street, and I walked down, intending to go to the quay first, as I thought I had plenty of time but in going down Grey Street I thought I would not have sufficient time, and cut through High Bridge. I went to the station and arrived there early [*see Plate 17*].

When I got into the booking hall I did not see anyone whom I knew. When I went to the ticket office I saw Nisbet and he said 'Good Morning' and I said 'Good Morning.' I would not have spoken to him if he had not spoken to me. I then got a return ticket for Stannington. I have known Nisbet for several years, but I was never intimate with him. He was just a casual acquaintance. I knew he was on the quay, but what he was or what he was employed in I did not know.

After buying my ticket I went to the bookstall to buy a *Manchester Sporting Chronicle*. From there I went to the refreshment room, and had some refreshments. I looked at the clock. It was about twenty minutes past ten.

I came out and walked round to take my seat. Whether I went through the number 4 gateway or behind the cigar store or in front of it I will not swear, but I know I went to the lavatory of platform 8. I never saw the deceased man again after he had left the booking hall. It is true that I got my ticket just after him, but to the best of my knowledge, I was never in his company or near him after that. I then went through the connecting way and took my seat. The train was a good long way up the platform.

By the time I had taken my seat the train was just about to start. After I had taken my seat I put my coat on the rack. I read my paper. I looked at the racing news and had a look at the programme. It was the Grand National day and to a racing man the information in the paper was extremely interesting.

I know I got in near the end of the train. I think about two compartments away from one that had a reserved ticket on the window. I did not notice the train draw up at Stannington. Nor do I think I noticed any of the stations after leaving Newcastle until I was surprised to

Tuesday, 5 July 1910 – Dickman's Evidence

find the train swerving, and then I knew it was Morpeth, for there is a swerve outside the station. It woke me up, as it were.

When we got to Morpeth I noticed some porters. We stopped a long way up the platform, past the refreshment room. I went out at the south end of the station, and took my ticket out of my waistcoat pocket and gave it to the collector. I do not know whether I had my coat over my arm or over my shoulder. I again put my hand into my waistcoat pocket and took out some coppers. I gave the collector two and a half pence and said 'two and a half pence is the correct fare' or words to that effect.

When I got out of the station I considered whether to go back to Stannington by train, but had I got out at Stannington I should have walked from the Dovecot pit to Morpeth station.

I went down and turned onto the Newcastle road. This is the main road and goes towards Stannington but to go towards Dovecot you turn off to the right. I went down the road and was almost within sight of the drift. I had walked for half an hour or more. I do not know the name of the village, but there are some houses known as Clifton.

I think it may have been a little way past Catchbourne. As I had just got past these houses I was taken very ill. I had a very bad seizure. I think it was diarrhoea, but when I tried to relieve myself I could not. I got over a hedge. This, from the great amount of strain, brought on another complaint. I never told Weddell about this because I did not wish to discuss my infirmities. By the other complaint I mean piles, which I have been troubled with for about twelve to fifteen years. Whilst I have been in prison I have been treated for them.

> After some time I got some relief. I got my coat out and lay down for a short time. I felt very ill. I should think, on and off, that I lay down about an hour and a half. I was in such a state that I thought it better to get back to Morpeth and get the train home. I went back towards Morpeth station, but I could not walk very quickly.
>
> I should think it was twenty minutes past one when I was on the platform. I put my coat on and went out of the east side of the station. I went out to cool myself down a little.
>
> I went a short way up the bank. I met no one that I knew. It struck me that I would go down and see if Mr Hogg was in the Newcastle Arms, and on going down I met Elliott and his friend. I stopped and asked them if they had any information about the big race. After stopping to speak to them I thought I had better return and catch the 1.40, which I did. All this happened on March 18th.

Dickman then went on to talk of Inspector Tait's visit to his home, and his subsequent arrest at the police station. He then turned to the identification parade where Percival Hall had picked him out.

> I remember the witness Hall being brought in. I was standing about the middle of the men who were put up for identification. He came and he talked, and he went three or four times past me, and then he was walking away. There was a stout officer who sort of jokingly dashed up and, it seemed to me, said; 'You cannot get out of here without choosing someone or making a selection.' The man was very reluctant to do so, and if he had not been practically intimidated into it, he would have made none.

Turning to the matter of the gun sent to Miss Hymen's shop, Dickman said he had sent back the revolver back and had never even opened the

Tuesday, 5 July 1910 – Dickman's Evidence

package. He then went on to the matter of the various bank accounts, pointing out that he had held an account at Lambton's Bank in Grey Street for as long as ten years. He had used many of their canvas bags as purses and once one was worn out, he would simply replace it. Finally, Dickman confirmed that he was not short of cash. The money he had had on him at the time of his arrest was his reserve fund to start betting again, once the flat season started.

Dickman had given his defence. It was now up to the prosecution to test it.

Chapter 17

Tuesday, 5 July 1910 – Cross Examination

Some of what was in store for John Dickman can be determined from the very first question he was asked. Mr Edward Tindal Atkinson began,

> 'You say you knew the deceased man?'
>
> 'I knew the deceased man; but if I had been asked off-hand what his name was, I could not have told you.'

Mr Atkinson continued,

> 'Did you not know his name?'
>
> 'No, if anyone had said to me "Do you know Nisbet" after a description, I would have known the man.'
>
> 'I do not understand you. Did you know his name, or did you not?'
>
> 'Yes, but if I had been asked off-hand, I would not be able to call that man Nisbet.'
>
> 'But you know his name was Nisbet?'
>
> 'Yes.'

Now it was time for the judge, Lord Coleridge, to add his own comments,

Tuesday, 5 July 1910 – Cross Examination

'You knew him and you knew his name?'

'Yes, if it had been mentioned to me.'

Mr Atkinson now re-entered the fray:

'I do not quite understand that. Did you know his name independently at that time of anybody telling it to you?'

'No, he was not an individual who was in my mind at all.'

'I did not ask you that. It is a very plain question. Did you know this man by name?'

'Yes, I did know him by name.'

'On the eighteenth of March, did you know this man by name?'

'I did.'

It was then Lord Coleridge's turn again:

'And by sight?'

'By sight. I knew he was a Quaysider.'

A total of nine questions, from a barrister and the trial judge, to determine if Dickman had known the dead man.

The questioning then moved on to whether Dickman knew what Nisbet did for a living and that he carried money on a fortnightly basis. That involved a total of fifteen more questions, but Dickman did not say that he knew what Nisbet's occupation was. On a more general subject he did say that he knew that wages had to be carried to the mines, and that they were usually paid on alternate Fridays. He had, after all, worked in the industry himself.

There followed some discussion about Dickman's visits to see Mr Hogg at the Dovecot mine before the questions moved on to the events of 18 March.

Dickman was asked to confirm that he had seen Nisbet in the booking office on that date and he confirmed that he had gone to the ticket window just as Nisbet was coming away from it. They exchanged greetings, but Dickman had not noticed if he was carrying a bag. From the ticket window, Dickman had bought a newspaper and had then gone to the third-class refreshment room.

After finishing his pie and pint, Dickman had left the refreshment room and headed towards the gate to platform 4. He was alone at the time and, if Nisbet had been walking close to him he felt sure he would have noticed him. In fact, he never saw Nisbet again.

The questioning moved on to Wilson Hepple. Dickman said he had known Hepple for many years and they had once lived close to each other in Whickham, but he could do little to weaken Hepple's evidence beyond saying that he must have made a mistake. Dickman said he had not seen Hepple that day and, if he had seen him, he would have travelled with him.

The questioning now turned to the journey itself and Dickman admitted that although there were people travelling in his carriage, he could not recall any of them specifically. People got out and people got in at various stations and there may have been as many as five or six people in the compartment, but he could recall none of them in detail. He also had to admit that, despite the massive publicity the case had received, none of these people had come forward.

There was a good deal made of the end of the journey, where Dickman alighted at Morpeth instead of Stannington. Dickman said that if he had got off the train at the correct stop, Stannington, and gone on to Dovecot, he would have ended his visit by walking to Morpeth. In effect, getting off at the wrong stop merely meant that

Tuesday, 5 July 1910 – Cross Examination

he would have done the journey in the wrong order. Asked to explain why he would have gone back home via Morpeth, Dickman answered that he liked the walk.

The discussion turned to Dickman's walk from Morpeth towards Dovecot. It was important to get the timings as accurate as possible. Dickman said he had been walking for about half an hour when he fell ill. He climbed into a field to rest and was there perhaps another half an hour before he managed to start walking back towards Morpeth and that took about another half hour, making an hour and a half in all. However, Dickman would have left Morpeth at 11.12am. Adding on the hour and a half he described would have taken the time to approximately 12.42pm and by his own statement, he had not arrived back in Morpeth until around 1.13pm. That left about half an hour unaccounted for. Much was made of this apparent discrepancy but it must be remembered that Dickman said he did not look at his watch whilst he was lying in the field and he was just guessing at the time. A man in pain, as he said he was, could easily estimate the time incorrectly.

The cross-examination now turned to Dickman's movements after he had caught the 1.40pm train back to Newcastle. After getting back to Newcastle he had a cup of coffee, which seemed to give him the relief he needed. He had arrived home at about 4.30pm and that evening had gone to see a show at the Pavilion, finally getting back to Lily Avenue at about 9.30pm. On the Saturday, he was out again during the afternoon and at one stage had visited the Turk's Head public house.

Dickman was now asked about the Isabella pit shaft, where the bank bag was found. He admitted that he may have walked down that lane once or twice in his life and knew that there was a shaft there but he did not know its name or that it was subject to flooding.

Asked about the blood on his glove and in his trouser pocket, Dickman said he was unable to explain it, but added that he had not used those particular gloves since Christmas the previous year. As for the stain on his coat, he had got some bicycle oil on it and his wife had tried to clean it off using paraffin.

Further questions followed on Dickman's finances and some of the ground already covered was returned to, no doubt to see if Dickman changed his testimony. Eventually, the questioning came to a merciful close and the defence case rested. All that remained now was the summing up from both counsel and the judge.

Chapter 18

Tuesday, 5 July 1910 – Summation

The summations began with Mr Edward Tindal Atkinson speaking for the prosecution and his speech lasted for about an hour (*see Plate 18*).

Counsel began by referring to Dickman having given evidence on his own behalf. The jury had had the opportunity of watching him, testing his demeanour, and listening to the statements he had made. To a large extent, his testimony had simply been flat denials of the main facts, sworn to by other witnesses. The jury would have to make their own minds up as to whom they would believe.

It was true that the case depended on circumstantial evidence but the jury must decide if all these pieces of evidence formed a chain and in this way they would decide, beyond a reasonable doubt, whether the prisoner was guilty as charged.

Mr Atkinson asked at what stage of his journey was Nisbet murdered? Was he murdered before Stannington? That was impossible, because he was seen alive and well at that station. Was he alive at Morpeth? There was evidence that he was not. If they believed the testimony of John Grant, who saw no one in that carriage, Nisbet's body must already have been underneath the seat. It seemed clear, then, that the murder must have taken place between Stannington and Morpeth. The only conclusion must be that the murderer got out at Morpeth and Dickman admitted that he had left the train at that station.

They had heard evidence that the man seen with Nisbet at Newcastle was none other than the prisoner. One witness had seen them together near the gateway to the platforms. Another, Hepple, had seen them on the platform and Hall had identified Dickman as the man he had seen climb into the compartment next to his, with Nisbet.

They had the testimony of Nisbet's widow, who swore that the man she saw, in profile, at Heaton station was the man now standing in the dock. The evidence, therefore, was cumulative and did not depend on one witness alone.

Counsel then turned to the time discrepancy and said that Dickman's version of events, if it were true, still left a half an hour unaccounted for. Then there was the matter of the weapons. Mr Atkinson stated as a fact that the person who committed the murder felt it necessary to brandish two pistols. He then completed his speech with a reference to Dickman's financial status.

It was now the turn of Mr Mitchell-Innes to speak on behalf of the prisoner. He put forward an argued and lucid defence. He began by asking the jury to turn their minds to proof. Any proof had to destroy all reasonable doubt in their minds before they could return a guilty verdict (*see Plate 19*).

Many of the circumstantial facts the prosecution had referred to had been provided to the police by Dickman himself. It was he who told them that he had known the murdered man and that he had exchanged greetings with him. It was Dickman who told them that he had travelled by the same train and that he had missed his stop at Stannington and gone on to Morpeth. It was Dickman who told them that he had paid an excess fare of 2.5d.

Mr Mitchell-Innes then referred to the identification evidence. Charles Raven had said that he saw Dickman and Nisbet walking together, but Dickman had said that there was no one near him as he walked towards the train. An attempt was made to explain this by saying that the two men might have simply walked closely together and Dickman had not noticed.

There could be no doubt that Hepple's evidence and Dickman's testimony were at odds. It was for the jury to ask if Hepple might have made a mistake. Hall had seen Nisbet get into the compartment

Tuesday, 5 July 1910 – Summation

first and may not have had a good sight of the man who got in after him, and it must be remembered that Hall's identification at the police station had been a rather reluctant one. As for Mrs Nisbet, it must be remembered that her testimony grew and developed. Originally she had said she could give no description of the man she saw with her husband but later it had grown to a certainty that it was the prisoner.

Two telling points were then made by counsel. First there was the fact that, according to the evidence heard, no one got out of the murder compartment at Morpeth. The other was that it was certain that two weapons were used. Was it not incredible to assume that there should only be one murderer using two pistols at close quarters? The reasonable inference was that two murderers did the deed and if two men committed the murder then the entire prosecution case fell to the ground.

Then there was the matter of the blood. The floor of the compartment was awash with blood and, whoever killed Nisbet would have had to force his bleeding body underneath the seat. Only small spots of blood had been found on Dickman's glove and in his trouser pocket and these could not be proved to be human. There was no blood at all on his boots.

The jury were being asked to believe, if Dickman was the murderer, that he then spent hours in the vicinity of Morpeth, knowing that his crime could be discovered at any time. He did not take the return train to Newcastle than ran a few minutes later, or the 1.12pm. Instead he caught the slow train at 1.40pm.

The bank bag was then mentioned and the fact that the guns used were not found with it. No weapon had been connected with the prisoner. No hoard of gold had been found at his home despite the fact that the police had searched it twice, even digging up his garden and taking apart his piano on one of their visits.

At the end of the speech for the defence, the proceedings were adjourned. The next day, it would be the turn of the judge to sum up the evidence.

Chapter 19

Wednesday, 6 July 1910

Verdicts have been overturned and sentences commuted due to misdirection by the trial judge. It is difficult to see how anyone could possibly dispute that the summing up delivered by Lord Coleridge was nothing more than a travesty.

He began by referring to Dickman's financial position at the time of the murder. According to the evidence presented, Dickman was, apparently, badly off and in need of money. He then turned to the fact that Nisbet was murdered and must have been murdered by someone who was in the train carriage with him. Had the prosecution proved that Dickman was that man?

First there was the witness Raven who said he knew both men. He had seen an account of the tragedy in that afternoon's papers and had immediately gone to the police. He had testified that Dickman and Nisbet were walking along together and, whilst not in conversation, walked as companions and not as strangers who happened to be walking in the same direction.

This is a curious thing to say. Dickman had denied ever knowing Raven, but there is a more important point here. If Raven had known both men why did he not either give Dickman's name as the companion or, at the very least, a description of a man he claimed to know, even if only by sight. Dickman's name was not given to the police until Sunday, when Hepple rang them.

Lord Coleridge then turned to Hepple's evidence. He could not have made a mistake, unless the prisoner had a double. If Hepple's testimony was accurate then the prisoner's account cannot be relied upon.

Wednesday, 6 July 1910

The next reference was to Hall's identification. Speaking of the reticence Hall had shown at the parade, Coleridge proceeded to turn it into a virtue. Hall had been reluctant because he knew that he might be putting a man into peril for his life. That was why he wasn't cocksure.

Cicely Nisbet's evidence too was increased in value. Whilst it was true that her identification might be regarded as unreliable because she had improved it, there was also the possibility that the more she saw, and thought about things, the more sure she became.

Coleridge now turned to Dickman missing his station at Stannington. It was here that the judge began to invent 'facts' for himself. He began by stating that the deceased was alive at Stannington and sitting with a companion stating as a fact that this was clearly the same man that Mrs Nisbet had seen at Heaton.

This is an astounding thing to say. Whilst it is true that it is highly likely that the man in the compartment at Heaton was the killer, it is also possible that he left the train at some stop before Stannington and someone else got in. There is no link of evidence, or identification, to show that the man at Heaton was the same man as the one at Stannington and to say so is misdirection.

Coleridge then stated that Grant had alighted from the train at Morpeth and had to be corrected by Mr Lowenthal who pointed out that Grant had joined the train there. When corrected, Coleridge commented, 'You are quite right. He got in and returned the same day, but whether he got out or in really does not affect what I was saying.' Yet the judge then goes on to say that this witness observed that the murder compartment appeared to be empty. Thus, it was quite clear that the murder took place between Stannington and Morpeth and the killer must, of necessity, have left the train at Morpeth.

This too is misdirection. If the location of the murder is correct, then the killer could have jumped from the train between those two stations. By stating that it was clear that the killer left at Morpeth, Coleridge is adding to the 'evidence' against Dickman who admitted that he had left the train at Morpeth and yet is ignoring the fact that no one got out of Nisbet's compartment at that station. It should be remembered that this was not a corridor train.

Coleridge then turns to the matter of the excess fare. He makes much of the fact that Dickman handed over his ticket and 2.5d with his left hand. His right hand was under his coat and a possible explanation for this is that Dickman held the bank bag under his coat with that hand. This may also be misdirection. If one looks at the forensic evidence we see that the spots of blood were on the left glove; the other spots were in the left-side trouser pocket. I believe that this, and the ticket evidence, suggests that Dickman was left-handed. Surely if this is the case, and he was hiding a bag, then he would have held it in his preferred hand and would therefore have tendered the ticket and money with his right. No one bothered to check this and, if Dickman was left-handed, then this was misdirection.

Coleridge then briefly returns to the facts thus far mentioning the location of the murder and that Nisbet was seen with a companion. He then turns this completely on its head and says, 'This result of that surely is this, if we believe it, unless we are to throw it to the winds, that the prisoner had a companion.' If anything, the evidence shows that it was Nisbet who had a companion, but now it was Dickman. Coleridge continued, 'Have the prosecution satisfied you that this companion was Nisbet? If they have then the rest of the case is not worth investigating.'

After turning to Dickman's own alibi, Coleridge moved on to the fact that Dickman's own statement gave the police a good deal of information that they did not already know. This, according to Coleridge, may well have been the actions of an innocent man but equally, it may have been the actions of a guilty man, who could not know how much evidence the police already had. If they had, for instance, known that Dickman had travelled on the 10.27 and he denied it, then this would look suspicious. A clever man who was guilty would therefore tell as much truth as possible. The statement

Wednesday, 6 July 1910

may be consistent with his innocence but it may also be consistent with his guilt.

Further misdirection followed when Coleridge turned to the evidence of the two types of bullet. Referring to the fact that two different calibres had been used Coleridge said, 'The first natural inference you would derive from that is that this man must have been attacked by two persons, each holding a lethal weapon.' Coleridge then went on to dismiss that assumption by stating that since only one companion had been seen with Nisbet, there must have only been one killer. The idea of two killers is instantly forgotten, no doubt because it simply didn't fit the prosecution case. Coleridge had an answer for all this. The clever killer had deliberately used two weapons so that the police would think there were two killers.

The summation finally ended and at 12.55pm the jury retired. They returned to court at 3.32pm, after a deliberation of two hours and thirty seven minutes. Before the verdict was given, the judge had more to say. He referred to the matter of the prisoner's wife not giving evidence for the defence. This had been referred to by the prosecution counsel, but he should not have done so. Coleridge asked if this had affected the jury's deliberations in any way. He was told that it had not.

The clerk of arraigns then asked, 'You are all agreed on your verdict?'

The foreman of the jury replied,

'Yes.'

'Do you find the prisoner at the bar guilty or not guilty of wilful murder?'

'We find him guilty.'

'That is the verdict of you all?'

'Of us all.'

'John Alexander Dickman, you have been convicted of wilful murder. What have you to say why the Court should not give you sentence of death according to law?'

Dickman replied 'I can only repeat that I am entirely innocent of this cruel deed. I have no complicity in this crime, and I have spoken the truth in my evidence, and in everything I have said.'

Lord Coleridge, having donned the black cap, then pronounced the dread sentence of death. Dickman, before he was taken down to the cells, turned to the body of the court and in a clear voice cried 'I declare to all men that I am innocent.'

Chapter 20

Thursday, 7 July to Thursday, 21 July 1910

Dickman had been sentenced to death. Soon after the verdict, Annie Dickman wrote to her local newspaper to defend her husband. She said that when he had returned home on the evening of the crime, he was perfectly normal in his behaviour and his clothing was spotless. She also suggested that the identification evidence in the case was unsatisfactory. In fact, she could not know, at this time, just how close she was to the truth, because soon some startling facts would come to light.

Disturbing news had reached the reached the Home Office and on 13 July, the under secretary of state wrote to the chief constable of Northumberland. The reply is dated the following day, 14 July, and should be quoted in full.

> Sir, I am in receipt of your letter of the 13th instant, and in reply thereto, I have the honour to herewith forward you a copy of a statement taken from Mrs Nisbet by my Superintendent, Weddell, today.
>
> With regard to Hall's identification, I beg to state that the Chief Constable of Newcastle-on-Tyne and myself have today seen both Hall and his companion Spink.
>
> It appears to us to be the fact that while Hall and Spink were waiting in a passage, which was fairly full of police officers in plain clothes, that some loose talk went on amongst these men in this passage, and that someone suggested to Hall and Spink to go round and have a look

in at the window of the room in which Dickman was then being examined, and that Hall and Spink did go round and looked in, but could only see the tops of some human heads.

Hall alleges that he was accompanied by a police office in plain clothes, but Spink is equally certain that they went alone. Shortly afterwards both allege that the door of the room in question was slightly opened and someone, presumably a policeman, who was in the passage suggested to them to look in at the man. They say they did this, but only saw the back view of the man, and from that view, Hall said he would not have identified Dickman as the companion of Nisbet on March 18th, as the back view made him appear a much more thick-set man. He did notice that Dickman had on a light overcoat, and the man he picked out later on in that day was wearing a similar one.

He further states, and is most emphatic, that the impression he got when looking through the door did not in any way influence him when he came to the identification, such as it was.

For it must not be forgotten that Hall's so-called identification has always been regarded as extremely weak. Both Mr Wright and myself have very closely examined Mr Hall and Mr Spink this afternoon, and we find they are both certain that neither of them could recognise the officers who they allege made these suggestions.

In this connection we find that the incident as alleged took place between 5.40pm and 6.00pm, in a partially lighted passage and that in that passage at that time there were at least fourteen officers of both the county and city force, and two North Eastern Railway police, most of whom were engaged in this case, and none of whom were in uniform.

Having regard to the inability of Hall and Spink to identify the police officer in question, we do not consider it necessary to collect all the officers who were probably there at that time. Three of the officers who were probably present are on leave and two more are sick.

Of course, if it be desired, we could parade the whole number in a few days' time. It is only proper to say that several of the statements of Hall and Spink are at variance. One of the officers, known to Hall, and stated by him to have been present, has now proved satisfactorily to us that he was engaged away from the office till some half-hour after the incident complained of.

May I be allowed to say that even if these allegations were true, as represented, that Dickman then was not in arrest, and so far as the officers in the passage were concerned, they had no knowledge that he ever would be.

This is an absolutely scandalous affair. One or more police officers encouraged two material witnesses to look at a suspect before they attended an identification parade. It matters not that Hall said he only caught a glimpse of the man. The fact remains that this one incident alone should have caused a commutation of Dickman's death sentence.

I also find this scandalous on another count. It is disgraceful that this letter from a chief constable clearly states that he does not think it 'necessary' to collect all those present in an attempt to identify the rogue officers. Nothing should have been spared in finding this man, dismissing him from the force and charging him. Even now the police were closing ranks to protect their own.

This letter also refers to a communication from the widow, Cicely Nisbet. She originally, had said that she could offer no description of the man in the compartment with her husband. He had his hat pulled down, his coat pulled up, he was on the far side of the compartment and sitting in a deep shadow cast by the bridge at Heaton station. Later, after giving her evidence at the police court she fainted and later said that she had seen the exact same profile and was now certain that Dickman was the man.

Unfortunately, this same witness had forgotten to mention to anyone that she had known Dickman for some eighteen years. Her own letter, a copy of which had been included with the one from the chief constable, read,

> I am the widow of J I Nisbet, to whom I was married about eighteen years ago. I first knew the prisoner, Dickman, shortly after I was married and then only by sight. I was never introduced to him, and never spoke to him.
>
> On March 18th, when speaking to my husband at Heaton station, the view in profile I got of my husband's companion did not enable me to identify him as anyone I knew. On giving evidence at the police court I never saw the prisoner until I had finished my evidence, when I caught sight of him in the dock. He was in the same position, and I had the same view of his profile as I had in the train, and I then recognised him as being the same man.

It was nonsense such as this identification and the actions of corrupt police officers on which a man's life depended.

These factors were, of course, brought to the attention of Dickman's defence team and they must have been greatly encouraged by them. Dickman also must have believed that now he had a real chance of showing that he had been wrongly convicted.

Immediately after his trial had ended, and Dickman had been taken back to Newcastle gaol, there had been boos and catcalls from some

Thursday, 7 July to Thursday, 21 July 1910

of the crowd who lined the streets immediately outside the court. Now, however, public opinion slowly began to change. A petition to the home secretary was started and it began to attract a large number of signatures.

The petition began by pointing out that Dickman was a family man with two young children. Next it stated that the only offence ever recorded against the condemned man's name was a minor offence, not against the person, for which he had received only a small fine. It added that those who knew him were of the opinion that his nature was not that of a man who would commit such a crime.

The third point made by the petitioners was that all the evidence was circumstantial and that the evidence was incomplete in many instances. Finally, there was no proof that Dickman had owned a weapon which he could have used to commit the crime and that the £17 odd found on him at the time of his arrest could not be traced to the crime.

Whilst people queued to sign that petition in various locations around the city, another court case was taking place. Nisbet had been killed, whilst on an errand for his employer and his widow, quite naturally, sought compensation for the loss of her husband under the Workmen's Compensation Act. Messrs Rayne and Burn, for whom Nisbet had worked for many years, showed the level of their compassion by refusing to pay out, saying that the deceased had not met his death through an accident in the proper meaning of the word. They also argued that the 'accident' such as it was, did not occur in the course of Nisbet's employment. They claimed that a murder could not be classed as an accident and the risk of being murdered whilst carrying wages could not be looked upon as a risk incidental to his employment.

The case was heard at the Newcastle County Court and compensation was awarded to Mrs Nisbet. Still Nisbet's employers would not accept that they owed the widow anything, and they entered an appeal against the judgement. The appeal was heard in London over two days, 11 and 12 July. The judges confirmed the original award of £200 compensation and also ordered the company to pay the costs of the hearing. In this respect at least, justice was done.

Meanwhile, other wheels of justice continued to grind. The appeal date had been set and would be heard on 22 July. Unfortunately, that would prove to be an even greater scandal that anything that had passed thus far.

Chapter 21

Friday, 22 July 1910

The appeal was to be heard before the Lord Chief Justice, Lord Alverstone, and Justices Lawrance and Phillimore. Home Secretary Winston Churchill, had referred the matter to the appeal court himself, the first time these powers had ever been used.

There were a number of grounds to the appeal. First, there was misdirection by the judge. Second, that there had been a comment by the prosecution on the omission of the wife of the prisoner to give evidence for the defence. Third, there had been a withdrawal of evidence from the jury.

The first and third of these involved the same point. That was that the judge, in his summing up, had dealt with the question of motive. Evidence of motive cannot supplement the absence of evidence connecting the prisoner with the death of the victim. If the evidence was weak, then the suggestion of a motive could not be invoked in its place.

The appeal went on to claim that the judge's summing up on Raven's evidence amounted to misdirection. It was proved, by the witness, that the two men he had seen apparently walking together were not in conversation. The judge had not put that fact to the jury.

Turning to the evidence of Hepple, the defence claimed that this witness was now old and deaf and his powers of observation could not be relied on. This, in fact, was a very weak argument as Hepple was certainly not as infirm as the defence suggested, but he had, by his own admission, seen the two men from quite a distance. The identification evidence he had given was given greater force by the testimony of Hall and if the latter's evidence was discredited then by association, so was Hepple's. The court was now aware of the subterfuge that took place at the identification parade and Hall's testimony was, therefore, discredited.

At this point, the defence stated that they had the letter from the chief constable, which they wished to put into evidence. This letter referred to the identification parade in which Hall and Spink had been encouraged to take a look at Dickman before the identity parade. It is quoted in full in the previous chapter.

The Lord Chief Justice, completely ignoring the fact that there was a man's life at stake replied that this was not the proper way to bring evidence before the court. The application was therefore refused, and consequently the letter was not admissible.

Percival Hall was, however, in court and could be called as a witness to give evidence. He confirmed that he and Spink had been taken to the police station in Pilgrim Street, to identify a man on 21 March. They had been waiting in a passage for some ten minutes or so when a detective officer invited them to have a look through a window at the man inside. They could see nothing and he expressed the opinion that it was ridiculous to expect them to see anything through the window. It was then that someone made the suggestion of looking through the slightly opened door. They saw a man, sitting in a chair, leaning over towards another man and apparently in conversation. The first man had no hat on and was wearing a light coloured overcoat. Hall could plainly see the colour of the man's hair (*see Plates 20 and 21*).

Some time later, Hall and Spink were taken upstairs to a room where the parade was to take place. This was perhaps an hour and a half later. When they entered the room they could see that the prisoner was still wearing a coat similar in colour to the one they had seen.

The defence then sought to put into evidence the letter written by Cicely Nisbet, in which she admitted to having known Dickman by sight for some eighteen years. Once again the Lord Chief Justice

Plate 1. Alnmouth station where the body was discovered.

Plate 2. The entrance to Heaton station.

Plate 3. Heaton station, the platforms. Note the overhang where the front of the train would be in a shadow.

Plate 4. Stannington station where Hall and Spink alighted.

Plate 5. John Innes Nisbet, the murdered man.

Station	Arrive	Depart
Newcastle Central		10.27
Manors		10.29
Heaton		10.34
Forest Hall		10.41
Killingworth		10.45
Annitsford		10.50
Cramlington		10.56
Plessey		11.00
Stannington		11.06
Morpeth	11.12	11.16
Pegswood		11.20
Longhirst		11.24
Widdrington		11.31
Chevington	11.36	11.48
Acklington		11.54
Warkworth		12.00
Alnmouth	12.06	12.11

Plate 6. The train timetable.

Left: **Plate 7.** John Alexander Dickman, the accused.

Below: **Plate 8.** Gosforth police station.

Plate 9. Pilgrim Street police station.

Plate 10. An aerial view of Newcastle gaol.

Engine

| Luggage |
| Bruce |
| Hall and Spink |
| Nisbet |

| Grant |
| 1st Class |
| 1st Class |
| |

| |
| |
| Hepple |
| |

| |
| |
| Wilkinson |

Left: **Plate 11.** An outline of the train showing where the various witnesses say they were sitting.

Below: **Plate 12.** The Moot Hall in Newcastle where the magistrates heard the evidence and where the trial later took place.

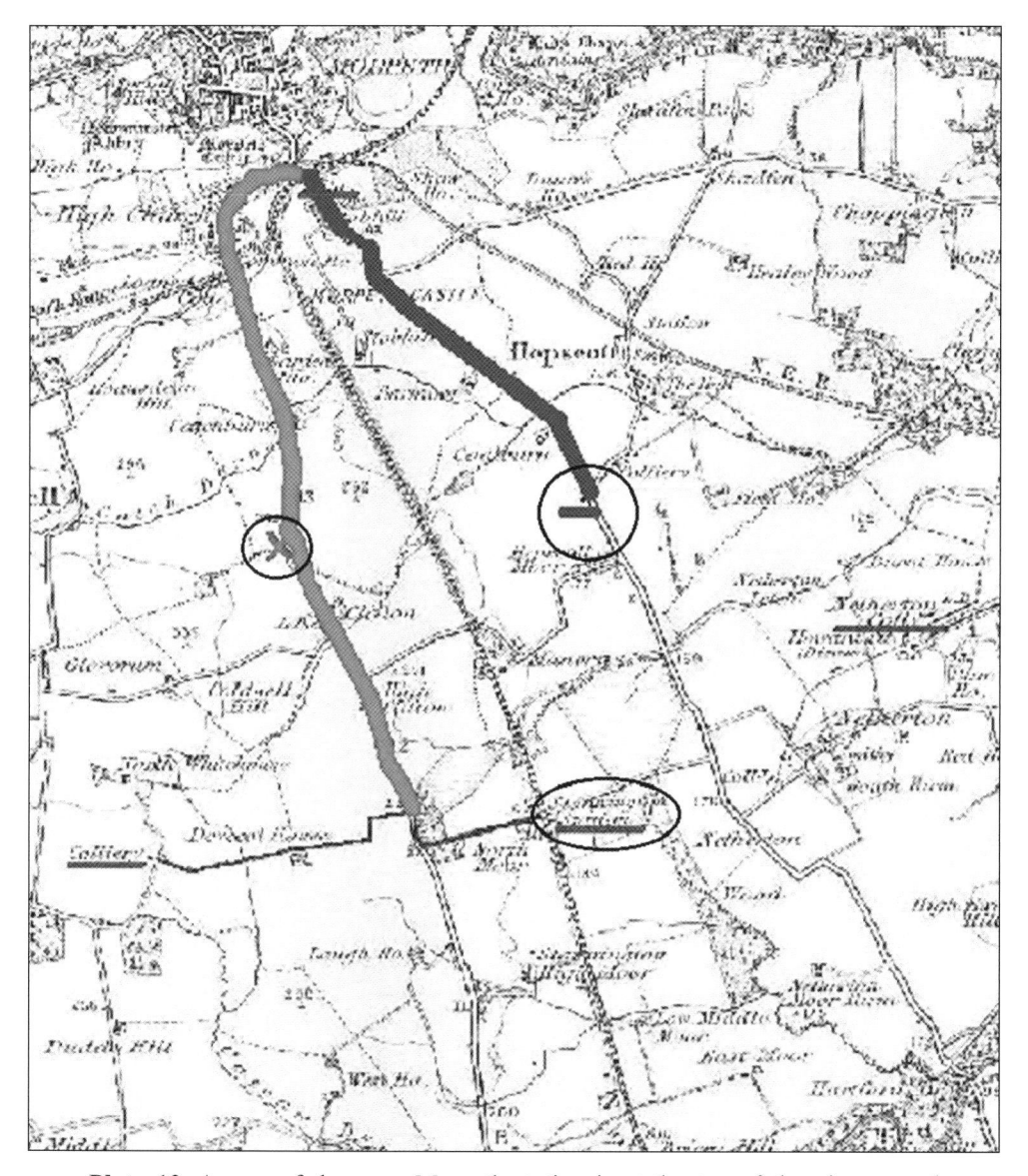

Plate 13. A map of the area. Morpeth station is at the top of the picture, and Stannington is at the bottom. Dovecot colliery where Dickman said he was going to, is above and to the left of Stannington. The other two marks on the map are explained later in the book.

Plate 14. Lord Coleridge, the trial judge.

Plate 15. Longhirst station.

Plate 16. Pegswood station.

Plate 17. Newcastle Central station. Platform 5 is at the far end, in the centre of the picture. Note that, coincidentally, the clock shows a time of 10.27.

Above left: **Plate 18.** Mr Edward Tindal Atkinson who led for the prosecution. This picture is from later in his career when he had been appointed as a judge.

Above right: **Plate 19.** Mr Edward Alfred Mitchell-Innes who led for the defence.

Plate 20. The corner office of the Pilgrim Street police station showing the window on the corner, next to the doorway, where Hall and Spink were invited to take a look at the prisoner.

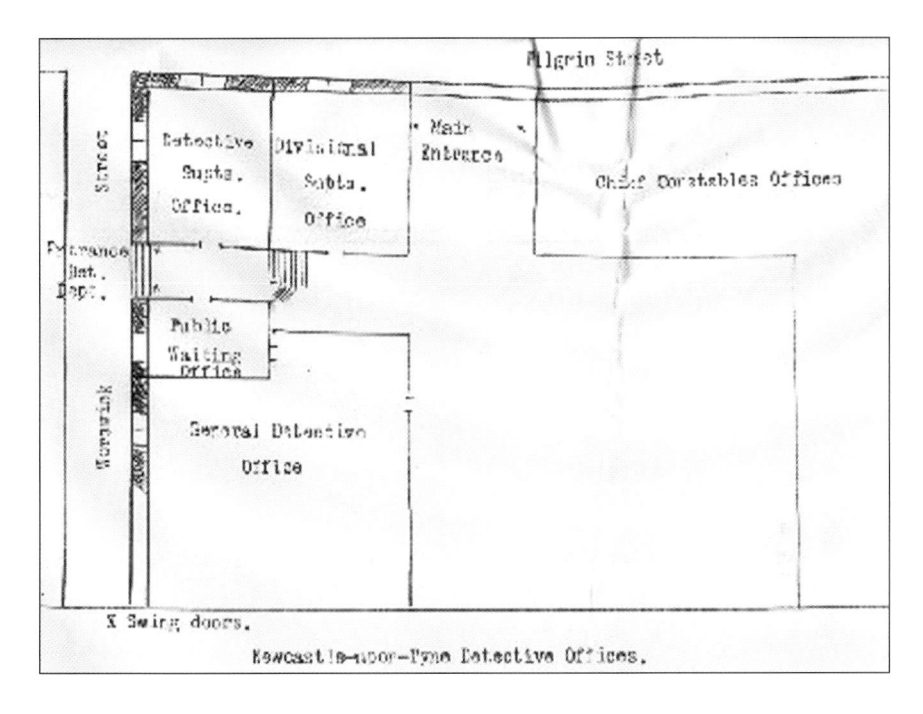

Above: **Plate 21.** A plan of the police station. Dickman was held in the superintendent's office on the top left corner, before the identity parade.

Right: **Plate 22.** John Ellis, the man who executed Dickman.

Plate 23. The outside of Newcastle gaol.

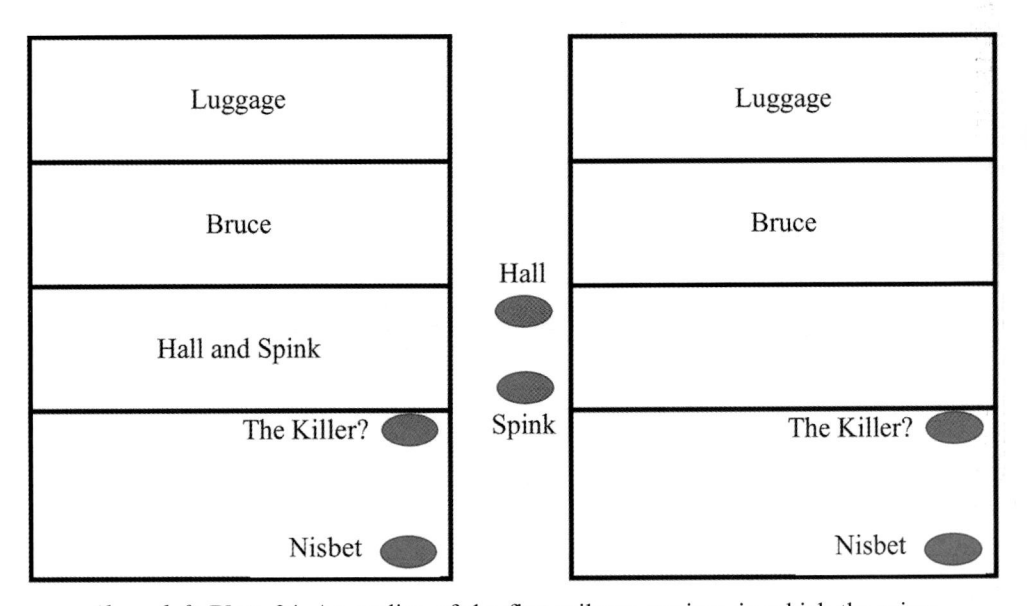

Luggage	Luggage
Bruce	Bruce
Hall and Spink	
The Killer?	The Killer?
Nisbet	Nisbet

Hall

Spink

Above left: **Plate 24.** An outline of the first railway carriage in which the crime took place.

Above right: **Plate 25.** The same outline showing the position of Hall and Spink when they alighted.

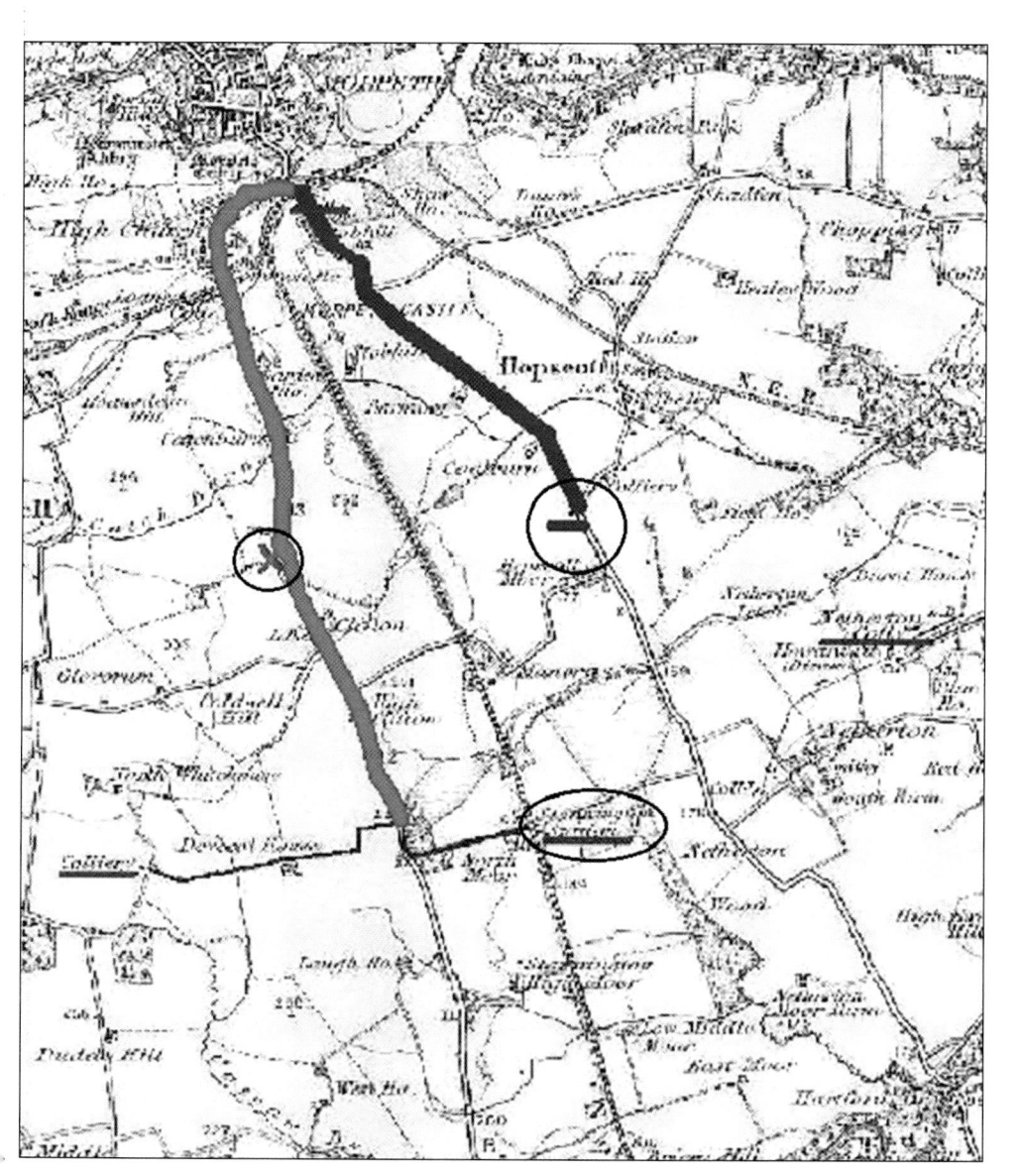

Plate 26. The same map of the area. The X marks the spot where Dickman said he fell ill. The circled line to the left shows the position of the Isabella shaft where the bank bag was found. The underline on the far right shows the colliery where Hall and Spink were headed.

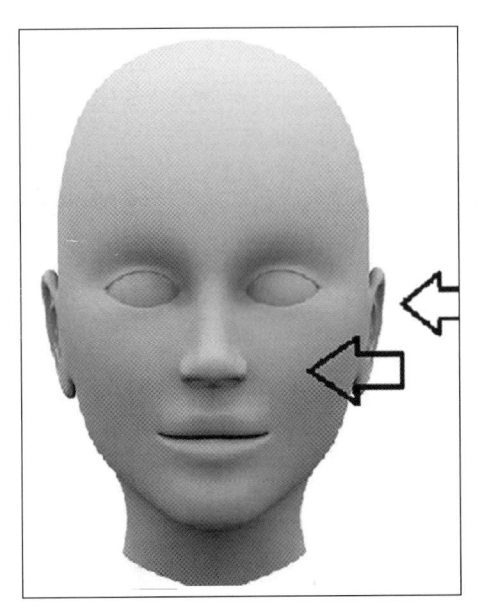

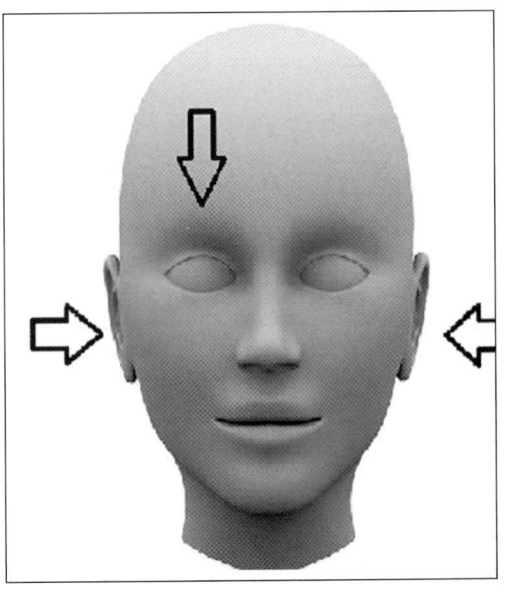

Above left: **Plate 27.** The wounds caused by the lead bullets.

Above right: **Plate 28.** The wounds caused by the nickel-plated bullets.

Plate 29. The summer house where Mrs Luard was found dead.

Above: **Plate 30.** The discovery of Mrs Luard's body by her husband.

Below: **Plate 31.** Harold Street, Sunderland, the scene of Herman Cohen's murder.

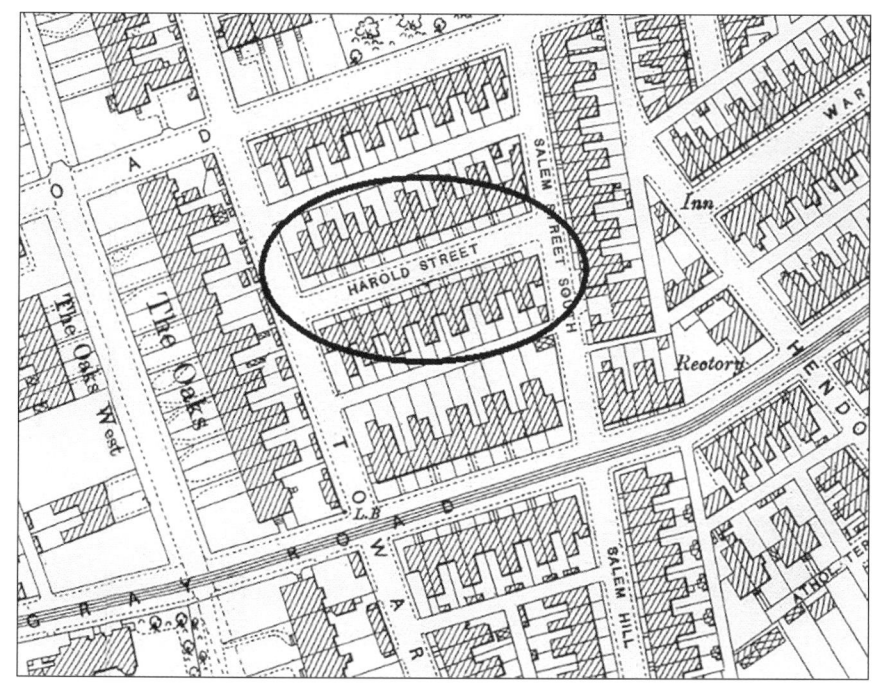

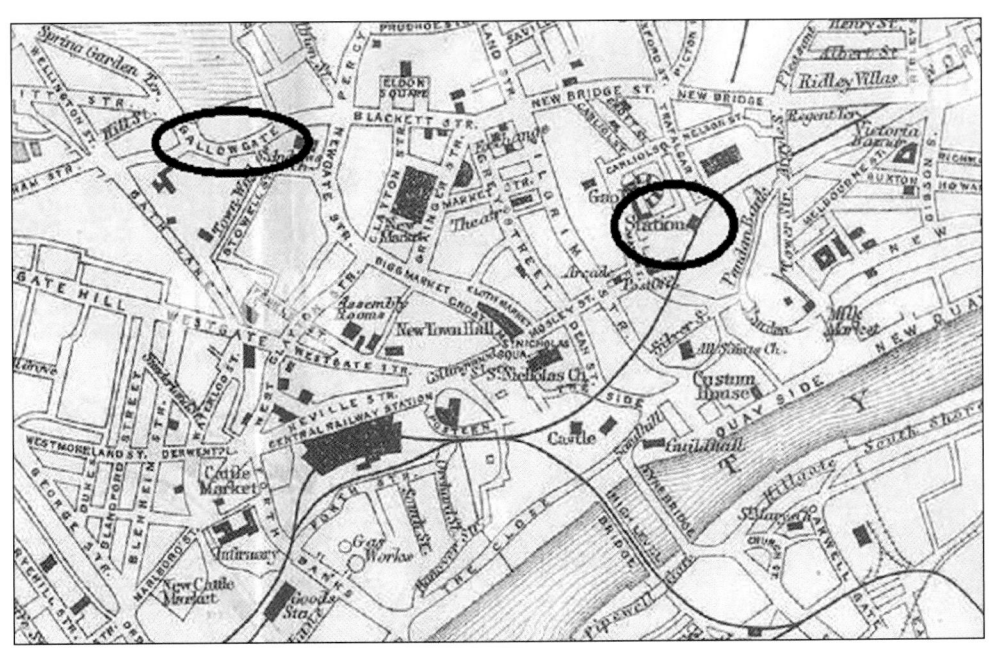

Plate 32. A map of Newcastle with the Manors railway station and Gallowgate, the location of Hepple's studio circled. The main shopping area is around the north of Pilgrim Street and walking to the Manors might make more sense than going to Central station.

Friday, 22 July 1910

originally refused to admit the letter but, Mrs Nisbet was also present in court so, after some discussion, the letter was admitted and read out, on the strict understanding that it should not be regarded as a precedent.

The defence then moved on to the subject of the bank bag being discovered in mid-June, pointing out that Dickman could not have put the bag down the shaft as he was in custody. At this point, the Lord Chief Justice showed that he had no grasp of the case whatsoever by saying, 'One would think that a man would have destroyed the bag instead of keeping it and then putting it down the pit. He had from March to June to dispose of it.'

This really does defy belief. In the first place, the justices were dismissing all thoughts of Dickman possibly being wrongly convicted, but their lack of understanding was staggering. Dickman had been arrested on 21 March and these out-of-touch judges were claiming that he could have disposed of it any time up to mid-June. No doubt the governor of Newcastle gaol let him out on day release so that he could do so! Don't forget that there had been two inspections of the shaft between the murder and the date the bag was actually found.

The defence asked that the original trial should be declared null and a new trial ordered. This should have been the very least that should have happened. No money had been traced to Dickman. No weapons had been traced to him. He could not have disposed of the bank bag. He had supplied the police, voluntarily, with a statement that gave them information which they did not have, which was surely the action of an innocent man, and the identification evidence against him had been largely discredited. Added to this, the trial judge had certainly misdirected the jury. The verdict should have been quashed and a new trial ordered. The judges, however, had other ideas.

The Lord Chief Justice began by saying, 'This case has given us occasion for the most anxious consideration. We have examined very carefully all the evidence before the sitting of the Court, so that we might be in a position to appreciate all the arguments.' He then went on to prove that they had done nothing of the kind.

The next comment related to the new evidence, which showed that the police had, in effect, helped to manufacture an identification of a suspect by allowing Hall and Spink to view him before the parade. The evidence of the letter was deemed to be irrelevant so the court would only rely on Hall's testimony under oath. The judges deprecated, in the strongest possible terms, this subterfuge and 'hoped' it was a rare occurrence. If they believed that justice depended on this single identification then they would not hesitate to quash any conviction that followed. Their conclusion was that, despite the fact that Hall's identification might have been slightly influenced by what had taken place, it had so little bearing on the rest of the case that it was impossible to interfere with the verdict because of it.

This is legalese at its very worst. Apparently it didn't matter that a key witness had been illegally helped by a corrupt police officer. That identification was not important enough to order a retrial. That by itself should have been enough to throw out the verdict.

The judges now turned to examining the strength of the argument that Dickman was the man in the compartment with Nisbet from Newcastle to Morpeth. The first piece of evidence in this chain was that of Raven who, the judges said, had known Dickman for seven or eight years, and Nisbet for about six. They omitted to mention, of course why, if all this were true, Raven had not named both men when he came forward on the afternoon of the murder.

The identification evidence was then taken up by Hepple, whose evidence had Dickman and Nisbet stepping onto the train together. As for the idea that Hall's evidence strengthened that of Hepple, the judges felt that it did not and even if Hall was totally discounted, it did not alter the strength of Hepple's testimony.

Having said that Hall's identification could largely be discounted, the appeal court judges then proceed to put it back in the forefront of the case against Dickman. Hall knew Nisbet and had seen him get into the next compartment of the train, with a companion. There was strong evidence that Dickman was this companion, because he had

Friday, 22 July 1910

been identified by Raven, Hepple and Hall. So, in the space of a few sentences we go from discounting Hall's identification to placing it back alongside those of Raven and Hepple.

A few other points are then referred to, including the fact that the guns used were never traced to Dickman. That wasn't necessary. Obviously, one could simply assume that Dickman had owned them and had disposed of them after the event. Even the money found on him at the time of his arrest was blindly assumed to have been part of the proceeds of the robbery. The exact words used were 'Nor is the case at all weakened by so little of the gold and silver being found upon him.' One can only assume that if Dickman had had but one silver coin on his person, that would have been assumed to have come from Nisbet's leather bag.

The final verdict was that there was nothing in the appeal and it must be dismissed. The fiasco was over. The verdict and sentence were confirmed. Dickman's only hope now was that the home secretary would commute the sentence to one of life imprisonment.

Chapter 22

Saturday, 23 July to Monday, 8 August 1910

Public opinion had now changed completely. Thousands signed the petition for Dickman to be reprieved. Even gentlemen who had served on the jury that convicted him made public the fact that they would now have voted 'not guilty'. Meanwhile, there was yet another development.

On Wednesday, 27 July, Mr Hellier, the governor of Newcastle gaol received a letter. Signed C.A. Mildoning, it was a full confession to the crime. The communication was dismissed as just a crank letter from someone trying to have the death sentence commuted.

The public appetite for sensation had, by now, moved on somewhat, at least outside Newcastle. The story of another murder was now splashed all across the front pages of the nation. In London, a mild-mannered and ineffectual man had allegedly killed his wife, dismembered her, buried her body in the cellar and fled the country with his young lover. The search for this man, Hawley Harvey Crippen, had spread to the high seas and the police were chasing his ship across the Atlantic. It would not be until Sunday, 31 July, that Crippen and his paramour, Ethel Le Neve, would be seized by Detective Inspector Dew of Scotland Yard.

Dickman, meanwhile, languished in his cell and knew that the only way he would now escape the noose, would be by the grace of the home secretary. On 27 July, the same day that the governor received the supposed confession, Dickman wrote to his wife.

> My Dear Annie, I have your letter of yesterday, and am
> glad you have recovered your composure, and also that

Saturday, 23 July to Monday, 8 August 1910

you saw Mr Clark. Mr Snagg came to see me about four o'clock, and I understand he got permit, or was going to, for you and Kitty to visit on Saturday.

I am today sending a personal petition to the Home Secretary through the kindness of the Governor. I am still hoping and trusting that something or other will be disclosed, which will prove my innocence.

Give my heartfelt thanks to all those friends who know and believe in me for their kindness and help. More I cannot say or do, much to my regret.

For your own great and untiring efforts under all these heart-rending and benumbing blows, I cannot say all I wish, but to your own self and to Kitty and Harry my feelings are more and more deeply sunk in my heart for ever and ever.

On Saturday, 30 July, Mr Edward Clark, the solicitor who had represented Dickman, received a letter from the Home Office. It read,

Sir, I am directed by the Home Secretary to inform you that he has given careful consideration to the petition submitted by you on behalf of John Alexander Dickman, now under sentence of death, and I have to express to you his regret that, after considering all the circumstances of the case, he has failed to discover any grounds which will justify him in advising his Majesty to interfere with the due course of the law.

It was signed F. Blackwell. Dickman's fate was now sealed.

It is strange that it was Home Secretary Winston Churchill, who had felt that Dickman's case should be referred to the Court of Appeal, but he could not now find any reason to commute the death sentence to one of life imprisonment.

On the day before he was due to be executed, Annie Dickman released various letters to the *Illustrated Chronicle*. She also wrote a long, final letter on the subject.

> On the eighteenth of March, at a quarter or twenty minutes to ten my husband came to the kitchen where I was busy, and told me that if he were not back again by twelve twenty I would know that he had gone to Stannington. That was not an unusual event; it conveyed nothing suspicious to me.
>
> I saw him no more until about five o'clock in the evening. A friend was with me. He talked for a time and asked her to remain to tea. She declined, but could, if it were necessary, verify the fact that his condition was spotless, his manner was usual, his appearance normal.
>
> After tea, we all went to the Pavilion, no sign ever coming from him of any abnormal condition if such existed.
>
> On Saturday afternoon he accompanied my daughter and myself into the town, dressed in every respect as he had been the day before.
>
> So much for what I know. Now for what other people know. My task would be considerably easier had I the depositions before me. I have not. I wish it to be clearly understood that I am criticising, as an entirely impartial person, who listened carefully to all that was said.
>
> The first witness of any import stated that he saw my husband, whom he knew only by sight, walking along with a man whom he knew personally, namely, Nisbet, but admitted that he did not see them speak.
>
> Only a few days ago, I got off the car at the foot of Northumberland Street at the same time as a gentleman, whom I had never seen before and probably will never

Saturday, 23 July to Monday, 8 August 1910

see again. We walked together side by side so far as a casual observer could tell until we reached Worswick Street, because neither of us could manage to get out of the road of the other.

If shortly afterwards I had been found murdered would the fact of us having apparently walked down Pilgrim Street together have been proof that the man was my assailant?

The next witness was with another man. He proved the courage of his convictions and practically refused to take upon himself the very grave responsibility of helping to condemn a man to death.

His companion was described by the judge as being an important witness. Quite so, provided no pressure was ever brought to bear upon him from outside. If, however, it is true that he was invited to look through a window at a man sitting alone in a room, previous to going for his tea, and was after taken to identify my husband, his evidence conveys little. If he were induced to do this by the police, then every man present on that occasion ought to be dismissed from the force.

The next witness was the man who, I am told, gave information in the first place to the police. It is significant, I think that, if I remember rightly, one hundred pounds reward was offered on the Saturday, and the telephone call came through on the Sunday afternoon. I make no comment on him.

Mrs Nisbet, on the first occasion, I believe, stated that owing to the shadow thrown by the archway and the engine, along the seat, she was unable to identify the man in the compartment. Her husband was not in the part of the train she usually found him in; she had to look for him and hurry to the front. As the train stays only a short a time in Heaton station I cannot see that much time was at her disposal for particularly noticing anything.

On the second occasion, this lady positively identified my husband when in the dock as being the man she saw in the compartment. Now the man in the compartment, she alleged, wore his coat collar turned up, his hat pulled down, and never moved. Would it not have been more satisfactory to all concerned if my husband had been dressed as the man was dressed, before she so positively identified? An inch or so of a man's nose isn't much to go by is it?

My husband alighted at Morpeth and because he alighted, and because the prosecution say he is the man, it has been definitely stated that the murder took place between the previous station and Morpeth. Not one jot of evidence has been produced which even points to such a fact being absolute truth.

At the hearing before the magistrates, a book belonging to Mr Pape, gunsmith, was produced showing an entry relating to the purchase of a revolver in 1907. At the assizes, Mr Tindal Atkinson asked permission to withdraw this evidence. Where was the evidence of Bell Brothers, of Glasgow?

Now as to my husband's cleanly [sic] condition. The only mark of an incriminating nature was, curiously, in a pocket. Nine tiny spots of blood, contained in a space so small that when Professor Boland held up the piece of cloth for inspection, you could scarcely discern it between his finger and thumb. It may be that when mending his pocket, I scratched my finger. Further, the professor would not even say that the blood was human blood. Is the blood of one person distinguishable from another?

Saturday, 23 July to Monday, 8 August 1910

As to our pecuniary position, you will notice that no one came forward to say that we were in debt or difficulties. The only evidence the prosecution could bring on this point was my transactions and letters. As these were my private doings, they may be wiped out.

I could go on for a long time. I have, however, touched upon the evidence in chief. Does any of it conclusively prove that he was the man who committed the deed? Most emphatically I say 'No'.

The date of the execution was now set. Dickman would be hanged at Newcastle on Tuesday, 9 August. On the same date, one John Raper Coulson, who had committed murder in Bradford, would be hanged at Armley prison, in Leeds.

On Monday, 8 August, Annie Dickman and her two children went to Newcastle gaol for their last visit. There was a railing keeping the prisoner and his family apart and as the interview ended, after some thirty minutes, Annie begged that her husband might be brought around to kiss his children for the last time. The authorities, heartless to the end, refused permission.

That evening, Dickman wrote his last letter to his wife. In that, at one stage, he wrote, 'There is something still keeps telling me that everything will be made clear some day, when it is too late to benefit me. I can only repeat that I am innocent.'

That same evening, John Ellis, the executioner, arrived at the prison to make his final arrangements (*see Plate 22*).

Chapter 23

Tuesday, 9 August 1910

The last execution at Newcastle gaol had taken place on Wednesday, 6 December 1905, when Henry Perkins had been hanged for the murder of Patrick Durkin at 94 Newgate Street in the city. The one prior to that had been a double execution in December 1901, when John Miller and John Robert Miller were hanged for a murder at Cullercoates. On both of those occasions, John Ellis had been an assistant. Now he was to be the number one for the first time at this prison (*see Plate 23*).

Ellis had made his preparations. He had been informed that Dickman was 5 feet, 5 and 7/8s of an inch tall and weighed 155 pounds. Ellis calculated that a drop of precisely 7 feet would be correct. The execution was due to take place at 8.00am.

In his own book, *Diary of a Hangman*, Ellis gives us a glimpse into his opinion of hanging. He had been given the option of two dates on which to execute Dickman: Saturday, 6 August or Tuesday, 9 August. He had chosen the latter but soon came to regret it when he discovered that there was to be a double execution at Leeds prison, also on 9 August. He was now forced to decline and that job went to Thomas Pierrepoint instead. In fact, one of the two condemned men, Edward Woodcock, subsequently had his sentence commuted, so perhaps Ellis felt a bit better about things after that. In the event, the reprieved man, Woodcock, did not live very much longer, committing suicide in his cell in September 1910.

On the morning of 9 August, Dickman rose early and partook of a breakfast of porridge, bread and butter and tea. He was ministered to

Tuesday, 9 August 1910

by the prison chaplain, the Reverend W.F. Lumley, who urged him to tell the truth about the murder of Nisbet. Dickman made no reply. By his silence, he was protesting his innocence for the last time.

At around 6.30am, Ellis and his assistant, William Willis went to inspect the scaffold. After satisfying himself that all was ready, Ellis walked back across the yard, to his quarters to wait the appointed hour. It was then that he noticed a man, perched on a school roof, overlooking the prison. The execution shed was positioned away from the main building and it was obvious that this man, whoever he was, would at the very least have a good view of the procession as Dickman made his way to the place of his execution. Ellis pointed the man out to one of the warders, who wasted no time in informing the prison governor.

Whilst Dickman waited in his cell he could have no idea what was taking place inside and outside the prison. A crowd estimated at around 1,500 had gathered around Carliol Square. Police officers kept them clear of the prison precincts but the streets around the area were thronged with people.

The governor, meanwhile, insisted that the man on the roof had to be removed, and despatched a warder to order him off. The man, a reporter, refused to move, pointing out that whilst the governor had jurisdiction within the prison walls he had no right to order a man off the roof of a private building.

There was no way that the prison authorities would allow a newspaper reporter a view of the condemned man on his last walk so, in order to thwart the journalist, a canvas sheet was erected to block the view from the main block of the prison to the execution shed.

At 8.00am, Ellis and his assistant entered the condemned cell. Seeing their approach, Dickman buttoned up his jacket and offered no resistance as his hands were pinioned behind his back. Ellis then began to undo the buttons around the neck of Dickman's shirt when the prisoner suddenly announced, 'I'm not going to die with my coat on. I'm going to pull it off.'

This had never happened before but for some reason Ellis acquiesced and walked behind Dickman. He removed the leather straps that were holding Dickman's wrists together and allowed him to remove his coat calmly and deliberately. Once he had done so, the straps were refastened and Dickman offered no further resistance. He walked briskly and firmly out of his cell and along to the execution shed which was some was some distance away.

John Alexander Dickman never spoke another word. He submitted to the placing of the noose around his neck and was dead within minutes of the incident in his cell. The newspaper reports of the day stated that the execution had passed without incident.

At the same time as Dickman was hanged, so too was the man who had escaped the clutches of Ellis: John Raper Coulson. He was duly executed at Leeds, by Thomas Pierrepoint, assisted by William Warbrick.

In all, the year 1910 was a busy year for the hangmen of Britain with 16 men losing their lives at the end of an unforgiving rope.

Section Two

THE EVIDENCE REVIEWED

Chapter 24

If John Alexander Dickman Were Guilty

Let us assume, at least for now, that John Alexander Dickman was indeed guilty of the murder of John Innes Nisbet on that fateful day of Friday, 18 March 1910. What then must have been the events of that and subsequent days?

I believe we can assume that Dickman was telling the truth about his early movements that day. So, he would have left his home in Lily Avenue at sometime around 10.00am. He got onto a tram at Fern Avenue and alighted at the bottom of Northumberland Street. He began to walk down to the quay but as he strolled down Grey Street, he realised that he didn't have as much time as he originally thought, so cut through High Bridge and on to the Central station where he arrived with time to spare.

Dickman was, of course, carrying two guns and had tested at least one of them, probably the more powerful .450 revolver, two weeks earlier when he had caught the express to Morpeth and fired out of the window of his carriage. It hadn't been a particularly risky endeavour. All he had needed to do, was make sure he was travelling alone and fire the gun well before he arrived at Morpeth. Then, even if someone raised the alarm, he would have time to conceal the gun and make good his escape in the crowd before anyone could investigate where the shot had been fired from.

The first thing to do, now he was at the station, was to ensure that his quarry was travelling that morning. Dickman may have waited outside the ticket hall until he saw Nisbet or, fortuitously, the intended victim just happened to be in front of him in the queue. Either way,

Dickman stood behind Nisbet as the latter purchased his ticket and the two men exchanged a pleasant greeting.

Dickman knew that in order to establish an alibi, he would have to have a valid reason for travelling on the train. He had already established a pattern by visiting Mr Hogg at Dovecot on a number of occasions, the last being just two weeks previously, after the testing of the gun. He therefore had the choice of travelling either to Morpeth or Stannington. Morpeth would be tricky though. The train stopped there for four minutes to take on water and there were more people travelling from there. If one of the people waiting for the train were to get into the compartment where Nisbet's body would be, the crime would be discovered immediately. It made more sense to get a ticket for Stannington, kill Nisbet before the train reached that station and then walk on to the Dovecot colliery. If the body had been discovered by the time he reached that station, and Dickman found the place crawling with police, he had merely to present himself as someone else wishing to catch a train back to Newcastle. This would be some time after the crime had been committed and there would be no reason to associate Dickman with the murder.

Dickman duly purchased a return ticket to Stannington, not noticing that Wilson Hepple, someone he had known for many years, had been at the front of the queue in the ticket hall.

We cannot be sure precisely what would have happened next. Perhaps Dickman engaged Nisbet in conversation somewhere on the station concourse. Perhaps he did buy a newspaper and some refreshments, always keeping an eye on where Nisbet was, or perhaps Nisbet even accompanied him to the refreshment room. We know, from Hepple's evidence, that the platform number of the 10.27 train was not put up for some time, and that he reached the platform first and was outside his own chosen carriage before the two men arrived. Whatever did happen, Dickman was in time to walk with Nisbet, through the gates that led to platform 5, for they were seen together by Charles Raven, though they were not in conversation.

Getting onto the platform itself, Dickman was careful enough to walk at the far end of the wide platform. He had to persuade Nisbet to get onto the train close to the engine where the noise would smother the sound of shots. However, as they walked on, Dickman either didn't notice Wilson Hepple parading up and down outside his chosen carriage, or chose to simply ignore the fact that someone who knew him well might later be able to identify him as the man with Nisbet.

As Dickman and Nisbet approached the front of the train, they reached the first carriage. This consisted of four compartments. The one nearest the engine was a luggage compartment. The next was a smoker, the last two were not.

Apparently, more concerned that they should not break the rules and smoke in a non-smoking compartment, than he was about murdering a man, Dickman ignored the first compartment he and Nisbet came to. Whilst Nisbet stopped and announced that they would ignore the rules and 'make this one a smoker', Dickman walked on, almost directly past Percival Harding Hall who was standing up, his head outside the carriage doorway, plainly seeing Nisbet and his companion.

Dickman would have known, of course, that Hall had seen him. He probably did not know who Hall was, or that he was on a similar mission to Nisbet: delivering colliery wages, but he would be aware that he had been seen. Rather than abandon his plan to murder Nisbet and steal his leather wages bag, Dickman chose to proceed.

The train left Central station and Dickman knew that his next chance of discovery lay at Heaton station. In order for his plan to succeed, he would have studied Nisbet's habits and known that Cicely Nisbet, a woman who had known him for years, would meet the train there.

Dickman, however, had already made two very clever moves. By getting Nisbet to travel at the front of the train, not only would the sound of the shots be smothered, but Cicely Nisbet would have less time to talk to her husband and so less time to see his companion.

If John Alexander Dickman Were Guilty

Further, the carriage selected meant that the bridge there would cast a deep shadow across the carriage. All Dickman had to do was sit at the far side, in the shadow, with his collar pulled up and his hat down. That way, the chances of being identified were remote to say the least. The plan seemed to work. Cicely Nisbet had but seconds to talk to her husband.

Originally, it had been Dickman's plan to shoot Nisbet somewhere before Stannington, but now there was a problem that required a change in that plan. Dickman had been practising and planning for weeks and had previously alighted at Stannington a number of times. Perhaps he had seen Hall and Spink before and even if he didn't know who they were or what they did, he did remember that they got off at Stannington. Again, rather than abandon his plan, Dickman decided simply to leave the killing until after they had left the train, even though he knew he would need to pay an excess fare at Morpeth, possibly attracting attention to himself.

At Stannington, Hall and Spink alighted and nodded to Nisbet in the next compartment. Dickman tried his best to hide his face by hiding behind his newspaper. He must have been highly relieved as the train began to pull out. It was now 11.06am and Dickman had just six minutes to murder Nisbet before the train reached Morpeth at 11.12am.

Drawing out two weapons, Dickman fired at least four times into Nisbet's head. The man lay dead on the compartment floor. Dickman snatched the leather bag and threw it onto a seat nearby. He then pushed Nisbet's body underneath the only seat available, the other having hot water pipes blocking the way.

The train arrived at Morpeth. By now Dickman had hidden the bank bag beneath his coat and got the excess fare ready in his hand. His heart must have been beating heavily in his chest as he stood, waiting to leave the train, and seeing people waiting to catch it. What if one of them got into this carriage? He was lucky, none of them did, and the ticket collector didn't seem to notice him much either.

The first choice was to walk around the front of Morpeth station, go to the ticket office and purchase a single back to Stannington. The next train back to Newcastle, would leave Morpeth at 11.24am. That would mean that Dickman would have to wait on the opposite platform for just twelve minutes.

The second choice was similar to the first in that he would buy a Stannington ticket, but stay out of Morpeth station until a minute or so before the return train was due to leave. In that way Dickman would know that Nisbet's body had not been found. He could then stroll back onto the other platform and wait for the return train without fear of imminent arrest.

The third choice, and the one which Dickman decided was best, was to dispose of the evidence as quickly as possible. So it was that he left Morpeth station and walked around to the east, towards the defunct Isabella pit shaft, a distance of some one and three quarter miles.

We can assume that the walk would have taken about an hour. That would mean that Dickman would arrive there some time around 12.15pm. He would then cut open the bank bag, remove the gold and silver and then cast the bag with the coppers remaining, down the shaft. Dickman chose, however, not to dump the two guns he had used down the same shaft. Either, for some obscure reason, he hid them somewhere else along that walk, or he kept them on his person.

Dickman now had two further choices. The first, and by far the simplest, was to walk from the Isabella shaft to Stannington station. Instead, he decided to walk back to Morpeth and only now buy himself a single ticket back to Stannington.

We can assume that the walk back would have taken about another hour meaning he would arrive around 1.15pm. He was probably just too late to catch the train he intended to, the 1.12pm express and knew he would have to wait for the 1.40pm. This was why he decided to walk into Morpeth itself where he met up with the two men who discussed the Grand National with him.

Having finally arrived back in Newcastle, with no apparent hue and cry raised, Dickman had to hide the bulk of the money he had stolen, along with the two guns, assuming that he hadn't hidden them already. He then, eventually, went home, still behaving in a perfectly natural manner.

We must also assume three other things. First, that Dickman managed to commit such a brutal murder, without getting any appreciable amounts of blood on his clothing. Second, that Dickman managed to find a hiding place for the money and guns that was so secure that the police never found them and third, that Dickman gave the police details of his movements on that day that they had not previously known in a belief that some truth would hide the greater lies.

Finally we have to believe that Dickman ignored the fact that he had been seen by Hall, Spink, Hepple, Cicely Nisbet and others, rather than postpone his plan for a fortnight, a month or more. Do these ideas really fit the facts or there some other possibility that is more logical?

That is what we will seek to determine but first we must examine the evidence that put Dickman's head into the hangman's noose.

Chapter 25

The Evidence Against John Alexander Dickman

Even the prosecution and the trial judge freely admitted that the evidence against Dickman was purely circumstantial. No guns were found at his house, despite a number of thorough searches, one of which even included digging up his gardens and taking his piano apart. The money was never found, though the appeal court judges tried to suggest that the gold found on Dickman when he was arrested formed part of it. Nothing in the way of major bloodstaining on his clothing was found. Despite this lack of true, concrete proof, we cannot simply ignore what evidence that was given in court. We need to list it and, as far as possible, demolish it. We should begin then with a summary of that evidence.

Identification by Charles Raven

Dickman was identified as the man seen walking, alongside Nisbet, through the gateway that led to platform 5 at Newcastle Central Station, though they were not in conversation.

Identification by Percival Harding Hall

Dickman was seen in the company of Nisbet, walking to the head of the train. The two men were talking together and got into the murder compartment next to the one occupied by Hall.

Identification by John William Spink

Though Spink could not formally identify Dickman as Nisbet's companion, he did give a basic, matching description, of the man he saw in Nisbet's compartment at Stannington station.

Identification by Cicely Nisbet

She swore that the man she saw in the fateful compartment with her husband was most certainly Dickman.

Identification by Wilson Hepple

Hepple had known Dickman for many years. He testified that Dickman was in Nisbet's company, that the two were in conversation and that they got into the murder compartment.

Dickman Had Financial Problems

Letters from Annie Dickman to her husband, various loans, pawned articles and empty bank accounts all showed that Dickman was in dire financial straits.

The Firearms Evidence

It could be suggested, if not actually proved, that Dickman had been in possession of a firearm at some stage.

The Isabella Pit

Dickman knew that this pit shaft would be a perfect hiding place for the empty bank bag.

The Practice Shooting on 4 March

There was evidence that someone had tested a gun two weeks before the murder and Dickman himself confirmed that he had last made the trip to Dovecot and Mr Hogg on 4 March.

Dickman's Alibi

This was weak to say the least and the prosecution view of events fitted the timetable much better.

The Staining Evidence

Bloodstains were found on certain items of Dickman's clothing and there was a large stain on an overcoat, which had been cleaned by means of paraffin.

All of these strands of evidence will now be examined in the next few chapters. Before it is, however, one must remember that in a British court, a man is assumed to be innocent and guilt must be proved beyond a reasonable doubt. The case against Dickman was always weak. If we can weaken it still further, will we then be able to say, with certainty, that the case against him was proved beyond that reasonable doubt?

Chapter 26

The Identification Evidence

As we have seen, there were, in effect, five witnesses who supplied some form of identification evidence at the trial of John Dickman. In, arguably, order of importance they are Wilson Hepple, Cicely Elizabeth Nisbet, Percival Harding Hall, Charles Raven and John William Spink. We shall examine this evidence in reverse order of that importance.

John William Spink

Spink was 23 years old at the time of the murder of John Nisbet and lived, with his parents, John Kitson Spink and Mary Ann Spink, at 51 Highbury. The family had moved there in November 1904, their previous address being 5 Poplar Crescent, Gateshead.

At Newcastle station, John Spink was sitting in the carriage and saw nothing of Nisbet's approach with his companion. The only time he saw this companion was at Stannington station as he and Hall alighted. Assuming that it was indeed the same man Hall had reported seeing with Nisbet at Newcastle, Spink could give very little information. What information he did give, must be regarded as suspect.

At the trial, Spink stated that he and Hall got off the train and both put their bags down. They then had to wait for the train to pull out before they could cross the railway line and continue on to the Netherton colliery to deliver the wages.

Nisbet was in the compartment to the rear of the one Spink had vacated and as he and Hall waited, Spink saw Nisbet on the far side from the platform. He was facing the engine. Nisbet nodded to him and Spink nodded back. The other man in the compartment was sitting opposite to Nisbet, meaning that he had his back to the engine. Spink saw that this man had a dark moustache and wore a black felt hat. He was unable to pick Dickman out at the identity parade but stated that the prisoner looked similar to the man he had seen in the train.

Consider, though, the possible positions of the four people involved. The very best position Spink could have had is shown in the drawing on the next page. From this vantage point he could indeed have seen Nisbet and nodded to him but it would be impossible for him to see at all clearly, the man with his back to the engine.

This point was made by Mr Mitchell-Innes at the trial, asking Spink if he saw Nisbet, and therefore his companion, before or after the train was moving. At the magistrates' court, Spink had said, 'I noticed the train passing out from the station on its journey. I then saw Nisbet.' Spink now said that he saw Nisbet both as the train was moving and whilst he and Hall were waiting for it to do so (*see Plates 24 and 25*).

Whatever the truth of this, there is little doubt that Spink would have had very little opportunity to view the man in the carriage with Nisbet. If we add to that the fact that this man held up a newspaper and the description was so vague as to fit half the men in Newcastle, we can discount any identification evidence from Spink and his testimony added nothing to the prosecution case against Dickman.

Charles Raven

The evidence of Charles Raven has partly been covered by Annie Dickman in her final letter to the press, just before her husband was executed. All it amounts to is that a man, who Raven believed to be Dickman, was walking close to Nisbet as he approached platform 5 at the station.

Even if this evidence is 100 per cent accurate, Raven admitted that he did not see the two men in conversation, so it does nothing to

The Identification Evidence

prove Dickman's guilt. At best it would be a one of a chain of events putting the two men in each other's company, but does it actually mesh with that of the more important identification witnesses?

Raven stated that his sighting of the two men took place at about 10.20am, that is some seven minutes before the train was due to leave and we know that it did leave on time.

Both Percival Hall and Wilson Hepple said that they had seen the two men together a minute or so before the train left. Indeed, their testimony suggests, that as Nisbet and his companion climbed onto the train, it was just about to leave. This means that if Raven, Hall and Hepple are all correct, it took Nisbet and Dickman some seven minutes to walk to the first carriage of the train and select the compartment where the murder took place.

Assuming a normal strolling speed of a couple of miles an hour, seven minutes would equate, roughly, to a distance of about 400 yards or almost a quarter of a mile. Are we to assume that the compartment was almost a quarter of a mile from the entrance to platform 5?

In fact, Raven's timings simply do not match with those of Hall and Hepple. It is my belief that Raven may well have seen two men fitting the descriptions of the suspect and victim, but this was too early to be the same two men positively identified by Hepple and Hall. Raven's testimony goes no way to proving Dickman's guilt, and can therefore be discounted.

Percival Harding Hall

Percival Hall was 29 years old at the time Nisbet was murdered, having been born in the summer of 1880. His parents were John Percival and Isabella Hall and at the time of Hall's birth, they were living at 38E Burlington Road, Bishopwearmouth in County Durham. The following year, there was another addition to the family when a daughter, Carrie, was born.

In the autumn of 1903, when he was about 23, Percival Harding Hall married Emily Ada Lowes and, by March 1910, they were living at 20 Deucher Street, in Newcastle.

There can be little doubt that Hall got the best view of Nisbet's companion on that Friday in March. He testified that he watched the two men as they walked directly towards him and the companion, according to Hall's testimony at the magistrates' court, actually walked past his compartment, looking for a smoking carriage.

When he made his initial statement to the police, Hall said he would have no doubt in picking out the man but, at the identity parade, putting aside the subterfuge undertaken by one or more corrupt police officers, he was still unsure. He said, in his police interview, after that subterfuge had come to light, and before Dickman's appeal, that he thought that the man he caught a glimpse of in the office at Pilgrim Street, was more thick set than the man he had seen with Nisbet.

Hall's testimony raises yet another interesting point. He stated that it was Nisbet, and not his companion, who selected the compartment where the murder was to take place. Perhaps we are expected to believe that Dickman was fortunate enough to have his intended victim choose precisely the compartment that would be in deep shadow at Heaton station where Cicely Nisbet waited to speak to her husband.

We could, of course, simply leave it at that. Hall's identification was, at best, uncertain and duplicitous even before it was completely discredited at the appeal court. For now, we will merely say that Hall's identification of Dickman as the man he had seen with Nisbet was of little value, but we will return to this in a later chapter.

For now, we will only note that Hall did not survive John Dickman by very many years. He died at the age of 41 on Thursday, 6 October 1921. There was a notice published in the *Newcastle Daily Journal* of 7 October.

'Hall – 18 Churchill Gardens, 6th inst, aged 41 years. Percival Harding, dearly loved husband of Emily Ada (née Lowes) and son of John Percival and the late Isabella Hall. Internment All Saints Cemetery, Saturday 8th inst, leaving residence at 2.00pm. No flowers.'

Cicely Elizabeth Nisbet

There is something quite disquieting about the identification evidence provided by Cicely Nisbet.

We must remember that in all of her early interviews with the police or the press, she repeatedly said that the man she saw, very briefly, in the compartment at Heaton station was at the far side of the train, with his hat pulled down and coat collar pulled up, and that he was sitting in a deep shadow cast by the railway bridge. She also stated, quite categorically, that she could offer no identification of the man.

Those who contrast this with the sudden and certain identification after catching Dickman's profile in the magistrates' court, often point out that such a scenario is not trustworthy, and underline this when it is shown that Cicely had known Dickman by sight for some eighteen years, though she didn't volunteer the information until after the trial. She may or may not have known his name, but this is irrelevant. If she did know his name, why did she not say in court that the man in the dock was someone she knew? If she did not know him by name, she would certainly have recognised him the second she stepped into the witness box to give evidence, at the magistrates' hearing. Why did she not immediately say that she knew him, rather than wait for some supposed glimpse of a profile as she stepped down from the box?

The identification evidence of Cicely Nisbet must be regarded as uncertain at the very least and should probably be discounted altogether. Further, if other links in the so-called chain of evidence can be either discounted or largely discredited then this evidence alone is of no value whatsoever.

Wilson Hepple

Wilson Hepple was born at 90 Byker Buildings, Byker Bar on 15 March 1854, meaning that he was almost exactly 56 years old when Nisbet was killed.

He had various addresses throughout his life, being recorded at Brickyard, Eldon in 1884, when he married Elizabeth Hunter. By 1891 he was resident at 67 House, Back Row, Whickham but by the time of the next census, in 1901, he was living at Cauld Cottage, Low Park, Acklington. Hepple had two children, John who was 24 at the time of the murder, and Ada, who was 20. He also maintained a studio at Gallowgate, in Newcastle.

Hepple's testimony is, arguably, the most damning identification evidence. Hepple had known Dickman for many years and claimed to have seen him walk past, some eighteen yards away, and enter the murder compartment with Nisbet. There are, however, a number of points that we will simply mention for now and return to in a later chapter.

First, if Hepple saw Dickman at the front of the queue in the ticket office at Newcastle, why did he not make himself known at that time?

Second, if Hepple saw Dickman walking along the platform with Nisbet, why did he not at least try to attract his attention so that they could nod and say good morning?

Third, if Hepple's evidence were accurate, this would mean that Dickman, carrying two guns and walking with a man he intended to murder within the hour, would not have noticed a man he knew extremely well, strolling up and down the platform. At the very least he would have aborted his plan for that particular Friday, for he would have known that Hepple would be able to identify him. Are we to assume that a man whose senses must have been keenly attuned from the thought of what he was about to do simply didn't notice a man he had known for years?

Fourth, initial reports were that Hepple stated that he caught the 10.29am train. The train left Newcastle, on time, at 10.27am. Was

The Identification Evidence

this a simple error on Hepple's part, or a misprint in the newspapers of the day?

As I have said, we will return to these points in a later chapter. For now we will just say that Hepple's evidence may not be as strong as initially thought.

What then is the summary of the identification evidence? If taken at face value, these five witnesses would place Dickman in Nisbet's company at Newcastle station, on the train itself, at Heaton station and again at Stannington. They would not prove, conclusively, that Dickman then went on to murder Nisbet. However, it can be seen that the evidence of two of the stronger witnesses, Cicely Nisbet and Percival Harding Hall can be largely rendered as unsafe. That of Charles Raven and John William Spink was of little value to begin with, and that of Wilson Hepple may also be suspect, as we shall see later in this book. In summary, the identification evidence is weak and simply cannot be relied on.

Chapter 27

Dickman's Financial Problems

There can be no doubt that the motive behind the murder of John Innes Nisbet, was that of financial gain. The killer was after the black leather bank bag which he carried, containing some £370 in gold and silver, and was prepared to kill in order to get it. Therefore, whoever was arrested for the crime had to have an urgent need for money, and if it could be shown that Dickman had such a need, then that would provide the necessary motive for him committing the murder.

The prosecution tried to prove this need in four ways. First, there was the fact that Dickman was pawning items, a sure sign of financial impecunity. Next there were the two loans referred to in court. Then there was the evidence of the depleted bank accounts and finally, there was a letter from Dickman's own wife, Annie.

Dickman's Pawn Tickets

Three pawn tickets were found in Dickman's house at Lily Avenue when it was searched after his arrest.

One of the pawn tickets related to some jewellery, a gold scarf ring set with three brilliants and a set of cuff-links. These were left with Mr Kettering at Cush and Co, jewellers of Collingwood Street in Newcastle and were pledged on 14 February 1910, Dickman saying that he wished to raise money to go to Liverpool. He received the sum of £5.

A second pawn ticket was dated 1 March 1910 and was for a pair of field glasses pledged with J.E. Wilson of 12 Pilgrim Street.

Dickman had pledged the item in the name of John Wilkinson and had given the address of 180 Westmoreland Road. For those glasses he received just 12s 1d.

The third ticket, also for a pair of field glasses, was dated 17 March 1910, the day before the murder. Again Dickman had used the name of John Wilkinson, but this item was pledged with James Somerfield and Sons of Pink Lane. Dickman had received 15s for this pair of glasses.

The prosecution at Dickman's trial entered details of these three pawn tickets, to underline their suggestion that Dickman had severe financial problems.

The three tickets added together came to the sum of £6 7s 1d. Dickman claimed that he pawned items in case any of the men placing bets with him asked if they might have credit. He would then be able to produce the pawn tickets and use them to imply that he had his own financial concerns. The prosecution seemed to forget that when Dickman was arrested he had £17 9s 11d on him, a not insignificant sum in 1910 and almost three times what he owed to the pawnbrokers. It was implied, at the appeal court, that the only way Dickman could have acquired such a sum was from the murder of Nisbet, but over £370 was stolen so, if this was part of the proceeds, where was the rest?

Dickman's own explanation is at least as likely as that suggested by the prosecution.

The Two Loans

Dickman raised two loans from a money-lender, Samuel Cohen, who ran the Cash Accommodation and Investment Company in Northumberland Street, Newcastle.

The first of these loans was for £20. Dickman went into Cohen's office around 15 October 1909 and said that he would require a loan of £20 for about three months. He was told that the interest would be £1 per month. Dickman said he would consider the matter.

On 18 October 1909, Dickman returned and said he would accept the terms. The £20 was handed over and Dickman signed a promissory note.

Over the next few months, the £1 interest was always paid promptly. After the three months were up, which would be in January 1910, Dickman told Cohen that he could not repay the principle of £20 and wished to extend it for a further three months: that is to April 1910.

Once again, the interest was always paid promptly and the final £1 was paid on 17 March, the day before Nisbet was murdered. The balance of the loan, a sum of £20, was paid off in full, by Annie Dickman, on 9 May 1910.

The second loan, for £200 wasn't actually taken out by Dickman but, on his advice, by Mr Christie, for betting purposes. The transaction took place in November 1909 and a cheque was made out to Christie. He countersigned it and the cheque was paid into Dickman's own bank account. The transactions are detailed in the next section, on Dickman's bank accounts.

This second loan can be largely discounted. Although Dickman may have had a hand in organising it, the loan was Christie's responsibility. We need only concern ourselves with the original loan of £20.

In court, Dickman said that he had only arranged this loan as a sort of experiment. He wanted to see if he could borrow money and what the rate of interest would be, possibly so that he could later arrange the larger loan for Christie. The prosecution made much of the fact that Dickman never repaid this relatively small amount. This misses one rather important point.

Frank Christie, the man who raised the larger loan, signed the £200 cheque over to Dickman and it was paid into the latter's bank account on 24 November 1909, and the full amount was withdrawn over two days. On 26 November he withdrew £160 and on 29 November he withdrew the remaining £40. This means that on 26 November,

Dickman was in the position, if he wished, to pay off the original loan of £20 without any trouble. Of course he would be using another man's money to do it, but Christie himself stated under oath that Dickman eventually had the benefit of at least £100 of that money.

Considering all these points, the loan of £20 cannot be regarded as significant and does nothing to prove that Dickman had financial problems.

The Bank Accounts

During Dickman's trial, four bank accounts were referred to. Two of these belonged to Dickman himself. They were accounts held at Lloyds Bank and the National Provincial Bank. The other two accounts belonged to Dickman's wife, Annie. One of these was held by her in the Post Office whilst the other was at the Co-Operative.

Though a number of transaction were detailed, the crucial factor was held to be the balance of those accounts as they stood at the time of the murder.

Dickman's Lloyds account had a zero balance and was, to all intents and purposes, closed, though Dickman said at his trial that he considered it still to be operative. His account at the National Provincial Bank was 3s overdrawn and had been since 31 December 1909.

Annie Dickman's post office account held a credit balance of 10s 9d and her Co-Operative account was £4 in credit on the day John Innes Nisbet met his death. The sum total of the four bank accounts was thus £4 7s 9d in credit.

In 1910, few working class people held bank accounts and most transactions were carried out in cash. It is true that all four bank accounts had once held large credit balances and were now largely defunct, but then it must be remembered that Dickman's business was a cash business. His only real need for bank accounts was to clear the occasional cheque which he might receive.

Annie Dickman's Letter

On 25 January 1910, John Dickman was away from home, most probably attending a race meeting somewhere. On that date Annie Dickman wrote to her husband.

> Dear Jack, I received your card, and am very sorry that you have no money to send. I am needing some very badly.
>
> The weather here is past description. I had to get in a load of coals, which consumed the greater part of a sovereign. The final notice for rates has come in; in fact, it came in last week, which means they must be paid before next Thursday. Also Harry's school account.
>
> With my dividend due this week and what is in the post office I daresay I can pay the most pressing things, but it is going to make the question of living a poser unless you can give me some advice as to what to do.
>
> Trusting to hear from you regarding what you think I had best do, I am, yours faithfully, Annie Dickman.

At first glance that letter might seem to be concrete proof that even Dickman's wife was concerned about their lack of money. This was largely explained by Mr Mitchell-Innes at Dickman's trial, when he pointed out to the court that at the time this letter was written, Annie Dickman had £17 11s in her Co-Operative account and a further £15 0s 9d in the Post Office. The total sum of money readily available to her was thus £32 11s 9d.

Dickman explained this letter by saying that it amounted to nothing more than a minor argument between man and wife over who was to pay for what. Dickman paid certain things whilst Annie was responsible for others. Whatever the truth of that, Annie Dickman certainly had enough cash at her disposal to pay the necessary accounts if she had to.

Dickman's Financial Problems

At Dickman's trial, all of the above factors were used to show that Dickman had financial problems. That may well have been the case, but even if Dickman were in difficulty, that would not prove him to be a murderer. Added to that, the pawn tickets and the loans have been largely explained; the bank accounts could be said to be superfluous and the letter from Annie to her husband might be nothing more than a minor domestic dispute.

John Alexander Dickman might have had some financial concerns, but this alone does not show that he was the killer of John Innes Nisbet.

Chapter 28

The Isabella Pit Shaft

Throughout Dickman's trial, the prosecution produced various bits of information, to show a link in a circumstantial chain of evidence, that pointed to him as the killer. One piece of evidence was given somewhat cursory attention for, if the defence had seized upon it, Dickman would have most likely have been shown to be innocent.

The black leather wages bag that Nisbet carried on 18 March 1910 was finally found, down the Isabella pit shaft, on Thursday, 9 June, some three months after the crime. Dickman had been arrested on Monday, 21 March, just three days after the murder, and had remained in custody ever since.

The foot of the shaft, where the bag was eventually found, was examined three times before the bag was discovered: Thursday, 17 March, Friday, 29 April and again on Wednesday, 18 May.

If Dickman were the murderer then the prosecution version of events is correct. This means that Dickman did not fall ill after leaving Morpeth station and the time 'unaccounted' for could be explained by him turning to the east of the station, walking down to the Isabella shaft, and dumping the bag. If this is the case, then he would have done so on the day of the murder, Friday, 18 March.

The prosecution never suggested that Dickman carried the bag home with him, rifled through the contents at his leisure, made a return trip to the pit shaft on either Saturday, Sunday or Monday before his arrest, and dumped the bag then. We are, therefore, left with a limited number of possibilities.

The Isabella Pit Shaft

The first is that Dickman did indeed dump the bag on Friday, 18 March. It then lay undiscovered for three months and through two inspections by Spooner, the man who found it on 9 June. This is entirely possible of course. Spooner stated in court that clay and debris constantly fell from the sides of the shaft and other items were sometimes dumped down there by other people. That, though, is the crucial point. The longer the bag remained down the shaft, the more it would be covered by such detritus.

The first inspection after the murder of Nisbet took place on 29 April. If the bag was dumped down the shaft on 18 March, then it had been there just 42 days by the time Spooner made that inspection. Are we to accept that he did not spot the bag after 42 days but managed to do so after 83, when the amount of mud and other debris would be greater?

In fact, Spooner made a most telling statement when giving his evidence, which again the defence counsel completely missed. Spooner said, 'I saw a leather bag lying at the bottom of number two air shaft. It is the bag produced. I brought it out of the shaft with me, and it is now in the condition in which I found it. There were some coppers in it, and also a considerable amount of coppers lying all around the place where I found it.'

We have pointed out that the mud would have covered the bag within those 83 days and Spooner might have missed it on his two previous visits. Must we also accept that the mud did not cover the coins either and Spooner managed to miss these as well as the bag? He described a considerable number of coins scattered about. Did he miss every one of them on 29 April and 18 May?

The only other explanation is that the bag was dumped at a later date which means that someone other than Dickman must have deposited it down the shaft. The fact that Peter Spooner did not see the bag or any of those copper coins on two previous visits strongly suggests that the bag was dumped down the shaft some time after 18 May and before 9 June.

The map shown on page 7 of the plate section is a detail of one produced at Dickman's trial. It will be recalled that Dickman stated that after leaving Morpeth station, he turned to the west and walked along the road towards the Dovecot mine workings, but fell ill along the way and ended up spending some time in a field, just about where the X is marked, trying to recover. The prosecution, however, stated that Dickman must have turned east out of the station and walked down to the Isabella pit shaft. This shaft is marked on the map as an underlined dot between Coalburn and Hepscott Moor.

Of course, for Dickman to have done this he must have known two things. He must first have known of the existence of the shaft itself and have also known that it was disused, so that anything dumped down there would be unlikely to be found immediately.

Peter Spooner also stated that he and Dickman had once worked together, years previously, so they did know each other. They had also talked about the difficulties the company was having with the mine, but added that he could not say if Dickman actually knew where the shaft was.

When Dickman was cross-examined on the second day of his trial, Dickman admitted that he had, in the past, been along the road where the pit shaft lay, but he did not know that there was such a shaft, close to the road itself. He also stated that he had no idea that there had been difficulties in working the pit because of the water problems.

Dickman may well have known that there was a shaft in that area subject to problems and so seldom used, but even Spooner said he couldn't be sure if Dickman knew where it was. Their conversation about the problems, if it had ever taken place, had been some considerable time before the murder. These factors, allied to the unlikelihood of Spooner missing the bag and the copper coins for 84 days greatly weakens the suggestion that it was Dickman who dropped the wages bag down the Isabella shaft (*see Plate 26*).

Chapter 29

The Firearms Evidence

In this chapter we will not only consider the weapons used in the commission of the murder, but also the wounds inflicted on the dead man and the so-called practice shooting of 4 March, precisely two weeks before Nisbet was killed.

Four bullets were found, either at the scene of the crime, or in the victim's head. Two of these were nickel capped and of .250 calibre. The other two were lead bullets of a larger, .320 calibre.

Testimony on these bullets was given by Thomas Simpson, who worked for Pape and Co of Collingwood Street. He gave evidence at both the magistrates' court and at the trial. Before the magistrates, on 15 April, he stated that whoever discharged the four bullets must certainly have had two weapons. At Dickman's trial he stated, 'It follows that these four bullets which were found in the man's body must of necessity have been fired from two different pistols.' Simpson also testified that the nickel capped bullets would have been fired from an automatic pistol holding seven bullets whilst the lead bullets would be fired from a revolver.

When the early investigation showed that two calibres of bullet had been used, the police began looking for two or more assailants, a gang of killers. Once Dickman had been arrested, there could be no suggestion of an accomplice. The witnesses, who provided what identification evidence described Nisbet being with one man only. There was only one man with Nisbet at Newcastle station, one in his compartment at Heaton and Stannington. Only one man paid an excess fare at Morpeth. So, the hard evidence had to be tweaked to fit the new scenario of a lone gunman.

The initial suggestion was that Dickman must have used two weapons. However, later in this chapter we will see that only one gun could be shown to have been possibly linked to Dickman. So, if he only used one gun, then he had to have packed the smaller bullets with paper in order to make them fit the larger calibre gun. This theory was held to show not only his desperation, but also his meanness.

This is nothing but utter drivel. To begin with, packing smaller calibre bullets with paper is highly dangerous and the weapon used to fire them had every chance of exploding in the killer's hand. The Dickman case was looked at in the BBC series, *Murder, Mystery and My Family* where a firearms 'expert' again maintained that paper could have been used around the smaller bullets but he, and the television programme missed a most vital point and that is that the only gun which possibly might be traced to Dickman, could have fired only the smaller nickel-plated bullets, so the paper-packing idea would not work as the larger lead bullets would not even fit the weapon. There is only one possible conclusion. Thomas Simpson was correct. Two guns must have been used.

Let us now turn to the various wounds inflicted on the dead man. Evidence regarding these wounds was given by Dr Charles Clarke Burnham, at both the magistrates' court and the final trial. At the magistrates' court, Burnham stated that when he first examined the body, blood was issuing from Nisbet's mouth, nose and the back of his head. His right eye was blackened. The upper jaw on the right side was extensively fractured, as were the bones of the face.

When it came to describing the wounds themselves, Burnham served only to confuse matters at the trial by detailing the wounds in

The Firearms Evidence

a different order. We can, however, summarise his testimony on the five separate wounds.

Wound One

This was immediately behind the right ear. The bullet that caused it had just entered the skin of the neck but had not entered the skull. There was no injury to the bones below the wound. The injury had had no serious effect and the direction of the bullet had been straight inwards.

Wound Two

This was a large wound underneath the left eye. The bullet had passed underneath the nose and evidently onwards through the bones, puncturing the right cheek bone. It was caused by a weapon being discharged only a few inches away from the face.

The bullet had passed from the left side to the right, through the nose and Dr Burnham found a bullet in the temple bone on the right side. It had taken a slightly upward course through the tissues of the nose.

The bullet found, and which therefore had caused this wound, was a lead bullet. The wound was a very serious wound. It had caused a large amount of bleeding and shock but would not, necessarily, have caused death.

Wound Three

This was on the left of the forehead, over the left eyebrow. It was a superficial wound and a nickel capped bullet was removed from it. The wound showed very little signs of burning.

The nickel bullet lay underneath the skin but had caused no injury to the bone. The path of the bullet was downwards, towards the eyebrow. Dr Burnham stated that in his opinion.

Nisbet would have been lying down or prostrate when this bullet was fired.

Wound Four

This was just behind the left ear. No corresponding bullet was found. The bullet had caused a slight injury to the bone below, but there was no actual fracture. This too was a superficial wound.

Wound Five

This was two inches below wound four and so also behind the left ear. The wound extended into the skull and was a large, ragged wound.

The bullet had penetrated the cerebellum and the medulla and was found in the anterior part of the brain. It would have caused instantaneous death.

The man who fired this bullet had held his hand below the level of Nisbet's head as it had passed through the collar of Nisbet's overcoat. The injury to the cloth showed evidence of burning and its position corresponded to the injury in Nisbet's head. Dr Burnham stated that the overcoat collar must have been pulled up. The direction of the bullet was upwards. The injury was caused by a lead bullet.

One of the bullets, a nickel capped one, was found in the compartment where the murder had taken place. The other three were recovered from Nisbet's head at the post-mortem. The fifth bullet was never found and may possibly have been recovered by the killer.

Dr Burnham also described part of the scene inside the murder carriage. Blood had run down between the cushion and the back of the arm rest and on down the seat. There was also blood on the front and neck of Nisbet's overcoat and the other articles of his clothing. He wore just one glove, which was bloodstained, as was the other, gloveless hand.

The Firearms Evidence

We have further summarised these injuries in the table below. Here we detail the number of the wound, the severity of the wound and the bullet which caused it.

Wound	Bullet	Severity of Wound
1	None Found	Superficial
2	Lead	Severe
3	Nickel-Capped	Superficial
4	None Found	Superficial
5	Lead	Severe

One nickel-capped bullet was found in the compartment and so must have caused either wound 1 or 4. It does not matter which wound it caused as both were superficial. This makes it clear that two lead bullets were fired, both of which caused severe wounds and that two, possibly three, nickel-plated bullets were fired, all of which caused superficial injuries.

How are we to make sense of all these wounds in an effort to determine what happened in that railway carriage? Rather than a simple list of the position of the wounds, perhaps an illustration might be of more practical use.

On the next page we have two diagrams. The first shows the position of the severe wounds caused by the lead bullets. These are wounds numbered 2 and 5 in the above list. Is it possible to determine which of these was fired first? Well, wound five caused burning to Nisbet's overcoat collar. Since he would not have pulled up his coat after the first shots had been fired, it is likely that this wound was an early one. It is also likely that Nisbet's head was upright at this time.

We know, from the testimony of the various witnesses who saw him, that Nisbet was travelling facing the engine at the far side of the carriage from the platform. Assuming that he remained in this position throughout the journey until the moment he was attacked, then to his immediate right would have been the train window. Anyone sitting next to him would have, of necessity, been on his left. The two wounds shown are both indicative of an assailant sitting to Nisbet's left and firing two bullets into him from a revolver. Those combined wounds, according to Dr Burnham, would have killed him instantly.

If there had been but one weapon used, that would have been the end of the matter. Nisbet would be dead, probably lying back in his seat.

What, then, of the other three wounds, all of which were almost certainly inflicted by nickel-capped bullets, fired from an automatic pistol?

One of these could also have been fired from the left. The one behind the left ear might certainly have been inflicted by a single assailant using a second gun. This does not, however, satisfactorily explain away the other two wounds: the one over the right eye and the one behind the right ear. These are wounds numbered 1 and 3.

Wound number 1 was straight inwards and wound number 3 was inflicted whilst Nisbet was lying prostrate, probably on the floor. The only way to explain this away with a scenario involving one killer, is that this individual drew out two weapons. He fired two lead bullets and one nickel one into the left side of Nisbet's head, killing him instantly. Nisbet's body either then fell to the floor, or the killer pulled him to the floor in order to stuff him underneath the seat. He must then have fired two more nickel-capped bullets into Nisbet's prostrate form (*see Plates 27 and 28*).

Or could it be that there were two assailants after all? One sat to Nisbet's left, held a revolver to his head and fired two lead bullets into him. At about the same time a second man, sitting opposite to Nisbet, and holding an automatic pistol, fired a nickel-capped bullet into Nisbet's forehead. He then stood, and either voluntarily or at the behest of his companion, fired another bullet into the left side of Nisbet's head. The body was then thrown to the floor, landed on its

The Firearms Evidence

left side and another bullet was fired into the right side of Nisbet's head.

Two guns strongly implies two killers. It was what the police held to be true until Dickman's arrest when the facts were twisted to fit the preferred scenario. There are then just two possible explanations. Either Dickman had an accomplice or two other men were involved.

We cannot leave this chapter without considering the possibility that Dickman owned one or more firearms. Attempts were made to link two guns to Dickman. One of these involved a gun, sent in error by Bell Brothers of Glasgow, to the newsagent's postal box Dickman used for his betting business.

Henrietta Hymen who ran the shop from premises at 35 Groat Market, stated that the gun had arrived in October 1909. There can be no doubt that it was sent in error for shortly afterwards a postcard arrived asking for its return. Dickman next came into the shop some two months later, and asked for an address label so that he might return it to Glasgow.

At Dickman's trial, no witness was called from Bell Brothers to say that the gun had not been returned. It is impossible to accept that the police did not make inquiries at Glasgow to determine whether it had or not. If the gun had not been returned, then evidence would have been given by the prosecution to show that a gun had been in Dickman's possession. The fact that no witness from the firm was called probably indicated that the gun was indeed returned. Unfortunately, this was yet another mistake by Dickman's defence barrister. He should have made his own inquiries and called a witness from Bell Brothers to show that the gun had been sent back.

The only other attempt to show that Dickman had possession of a gun was the evidence of Andrew Craig Kirkwood, who worked for Pape and Co, gunsmiths. He referred to an entry in the firearms registry he kept, showing that someone using the name John A. Dickinson and living in Lily Avenue had purchased a .250 calibre automatic pistol on 8 November 1907. It could not be determined which member of staff had sold the pistol and no proof could be offered that this man was John Alexander Dickman. So weak was this evidence that although it had been heard at the magistrates' court, it was excluded from the trial.

There is one last point to consider. Even if Dickman had been the man who bought that gun in 1907, he would have waited two and a half years before using it to kill Nisbet, no trace of it would ever be found and, finally, there is no way such a weapon could have fired the two lead bullets that inflicted the two severe wounds. Dickman, of course, denied ever owning any gun of any kind.

Chapter 30

The Staining Evidence

Whoever the killer of Nisbet was, whether that was Dickman, alone or acting with an accomplice, some other lone killer or some other group of men, there had to be the consideration of blood.

Nisbet had been shot in the head five times. Dr Burnham described a bloodstained carriage. Thomas Charlton, the porter who found the body, described three streams of blood emanating from where Nisbet's head lay. There would have been blood spatter and the killer later pushed Nisbet's body underneath the seat. It is difficult to believe that there wouldn't be some blood traces on the killer's clothing, even if they were relatively minor. What then was found on Dickman?

Doctor Robert Boland had examined various items handed to him by the police. Boland had been given a pair of suede gloves, a pair of trousers and a fawn coloured Burberry overcoat.

The Suede Gloves

Dr Boland noted a stain on the palm side of the left hand glove. In fact, it was a small dark red smeared stain about three quarters of an inch by a quarter of an inch. After testing it, Dr Boland concluded that it was blood, but he was unable to tell whether it was human or animal. He was, however, able to say that they were of recent origin.

The Trousers

There was a stain inside on the front left pocket, which was determined to be blood. In fact this was a series of nine small stains over an area of two inches by one inch. The pocket was eleven inches in depth and the stains were between four and six inches from the bottom.

The nine stains varied in size with the largest of them being only the size of a pin head. These stains had been made within a fortnight of his examination which took place on 26 March.

The Burberry Overcoat

There was a large stain on the left side of the front of the coat. The cloth was darkened there. The surface of this area showed signs of rubbing and it smelled faintly of paraffin. Under the microscope Dr Boland detected droplets of oil.

When giving his evidence at the trial, Dr Boland said, 'Assuming for the moment that the stain was blood, it would be possible, with a material of this kind, to wash out the traces, either by water or paraffin.' There is no way this should have passed unchallenged. There was no evidence that this stain had been blood but Dr Boland had been allowed to imply that it had been.

That was the sum total of the staining on Dickman's clothing; a single small stain on a glove and nine pinprick stains inside a pocket. As for the large stain on the Burberry, not only could it not be shown to be blood, but Annie Dickman had said that it had been a bicycle oil stain which she removed with paraffin. She was not called to give evidence in her husband's defence.

Dickman had two coats, the fawn one referred to above, and also a brown coloured one. Dickman claimed that he was wearing his brown coat on the day Nisbet was killed. The prosecution, of course, claimed that he was lying and that he had been wearing the fawn coat.

Once again a crucial point was missed. The prosecution were claiming that Dickman had been wearing his fawn coat on the day he shot Nisbet and that later his wife used paraffin to remove a large

The Staining Evidence

bloodstain. However, Dickman was seen in Morpeth by Elliott and Sanderson and they said he appeared perfectly normal in demeanour and appearance. Would they not have noticed a large bloodstain on the front of his overcoat?

In summary, there was no bloodstain evidence to link Dickman to the murder of Nisbet.

Chapter 31

The Remaining Evidence

What remains of the evidence used to convict John Alexander Dickman? The prosecution at his trial freely admitted that all of it was circumstantial. What does it actually amount to?

The evidence, such as it was, consists of a chain of factors, that when linked together, led to a conviction and a sentence of death by hanging. These individual links are that Dickman did not come forward, he knew the dead man, he travelled with him in the train, he was seen by witnesses, he had access to a gun, he was desperate for money, he had blood stains on his clothing and he had no alibi for the time of the murder.

The identification evidence is weak to say the least. That of Spink and Raven is relatively unimportant. That of Hall and Cicely Nisbet has been shown to be unsafe. Percival Hall made a tentative identification after being assisted by one or more corrupt police officers. Cicely Nisbet originally said she could offer no description whatsoever of the man she had seen with her husband at Heaton station and then, more than a month later, conveniently recognised the profile of a man who had his hat pulled down, his collar pulled up and sat in a deep shadow cast by a bridge. She also forgot to mention that she had known this man by sight for eighteen years. We are left only with a possible identification by Wilson Hepple, one we shall return to later.

There is no firearms evidence. No gun was traced to Dickman. No gun was found in the searches of his house. The only possible link was the purchase of a gun by 'someone', who may or may not have been Dickman, three years before, a gun that was incapable of firing two of the bullets used to kill Nisbet, with or without the nonsense of packing smaller bullets to fit a larger weapon.

The financial evidence is also weak. It relies on three pawn tickets, four depleted bank accounts and a letter from Dickman's wife. Dickman's business was largely cash based. He had no real need of bank accounts and the letter from his wife was nothing more than a domestic dispute over who was responsible for certain household expenses.

The bloodstain evidence was a small stain on a glove and nine pinprick sized stains inside a pocket. The latter could not even be conclusively proved to be blood, and the former, although shown to be blood, could not be shown to be human. There was no blood found on any other items of clothing, including Dickman's boots.

The fact that Dickman's alibi was weak does not make him a killer. The alibi, such that it was, did not even play a major part in the case until the bank bag was found down the Isabella pit shaft. Only then could the prosecution claim that Dickman had turned east out of the station rather than west. Until this point they had no reason to doubt that he had turned west, suggesting that he must have hidden the money somewhere along that route. Only after 9 June was the alternative route of importance. Once again the goal posts were moved to fit the evidence.

There was no strong evidence whatsoever against John Alexander Dickman. Crucial factors were ignored. He acted alone so he must have used two weapons or packed smaller bullets with paper. He hid the bank bag down the pit shaft, so he must have done so on the day of the murder, as he had no other opportunity to do so, and Peter Spooner must have missed it twice. No gun was found so he must have hidden it somewhere else. Percival Harding Hall's identification was discredited but, rather than order a retrial, there was still the evidence of Raven, Spink, Hepple and Mrs Nisbet, ignoring the fact that they were all weak too. He had financial concerns so must have been desperate for money – desperate enough to kill.

These are not points that can be ignored. A chain is only as strong as its weakest link. The chain of 'evidence' against Dickman has been shown to be weak in so many places. It is certainly not enough to condemn a man to death at the end of a rope.

Chapter 32

Bogus Information and a Confession

Elizabeth Richardson was the wife of Alfred and they lived at 4 Juliet Street off the Scotswood Road. On Tuesday, 22 March 1910, Elizabeth was in Leazes Park, with her children. They were having a picnic to celebrate the birthday of one of her offspring. Elizabeth, like most people in Newcastle, had read of Nisbet's murder in the newspapers.

It was 9.45am and the family group were sitting, facing the lake, on the eastern side. There was a small shed or shelter there and when Elizabeth went in with the children, there were two men already there. The two men were in conversation.

'That was a clean job on the train.'

'Didn't the blood well spurt up when we shoved him under the seat. The bag is down an old air shaft.'

One of the men wore a fawn coat and a light cap. He was of medium height, had brown hair but no moustache and was of rather stout build. The other man wore a grey overcoat and a light coloured cap. He was of medium height but slight build. He had a dark complexion and dark eyes. He also had a mark of some kind either on his forehead or just above his nose.

The two men now noticed Elizabeth and the one wearing the grey coat jumped up and approached her. He asked, 'How long have you been here?'

'Not long,' she replied. The man then offered her a sovereign saying, 'I'll give you a sovereign if you will tell me how much of the conversation you have heard.'

'I have heard nothing.'

The man then asked Elizabeth where she lived and she, sensibly, said that it was nothing to do with him. Soon afterwards, Elizabeth left the park with her children and saw that the man followed her, but only as far as the park gates.

Elizabeth saw the two men once again, on 19 July, close to the cattle market. She wanted to take this information to the police, but her husband told her that it would be better to say nothing. In fact, once Dickman had been condemned to death, Elizabeth decided that she had to tell her story to the authorities, but only did so on 2 August. She then made a written statement but no action was taken on it.

At first glance, it seems that Elizabeth Richardson has solved our case for us. Her story underlines the idea of there being two killers and neither of them could be Dickman as he was in custody. There is, though, a problem.

One of the men alluded to the bank bag being down an old air shaft. This would mean that the bag was dumped just after the crime and we are back to accepting that Peter Spooner missed seeing it on two occasions before 9 June.

It may be that Elizabeth was simply seeking a little limelight from such a notorious case, but if so she failed in her quest. The story was given scant attention in the newspapers and Elizabeth never did receive her fifteen minutes of fame.

Whatever the truth, we cannot rely on what Elizabeth said and must assume that it does nothing to help Dickman's case.

Another possible piece of evidence did not come to light until many years after Dickman's death. In June 1925, a large handwritten document was delivered to the editor of *Truth* magazine. It purported to be a confession to the Newcastle train murder.

The confession was signed Condor and the author said he was confessing for three reasons. The first was that he now had but a short time to live, as he had been diagnosed as suffering from cancer. The second reason was that he had thought much about the effect the case must have had on Dickman's wife and family. His third and

Bogus Information and a Confession

final reason was that he objected to the way the police had handled the case.

Condor claimed that he was now living in Scotland but was staying with family at the present time. The confession began with pages and pages of diatribe against the police and their methods. The document is a rambling and disjointed affair but the basic story, according to Condor, can be deduced.

Condor claimed that he had been born in Canada of Scottish parents. He was now 53 years old and had an older brother and sister. His mother had died when he was 6. He moved back to Scotland around 1900 and took up a position as an insurance agent.

At the latter end of 1905, Condor married. In early 1909, he became a representative for a firm of book publishers and in January of that year, moved to the Newcastle and Northumberland area. It was then that he took up horse racing. He was successful at first and took a larger cottage, which was more expensive. Then, as with many gamblers, he hit a losing streak and began using his firm's money to cover his bets. It wasn't long before his employer found out but, rather than dismiss him outright, they ordered him to repay the money on a weekly basis or they would prosecute. It was now December 1909.

Condor concentrated his work in the Newcastle to Morpeth area and sold books to miners amongst others. They were paid fortnightly so Condor would travel to the pits on a fortnightly basis to collect payment for the books he had sold. It was on these trips that he noticed the colliery pay clerks with their leather bags. On these journeys, Condor almost always travelled in a compartment close to the engine.

On 4 March 1910, Condor had to run to catch his train and only just managed to throw himself into the last compartment, furthest from the engine. He found himself sitting with a group of men in a hot political debate. The year 1910 saw two general elections and politics was a topic of the day. Looking around the compartment, Condor found that he was sitting opposite a slightly built man, who he would later discover was John Innes Nisbet.

It was Nisbet who broke the ice. He leaned forward and said, 'Excuse me, but aren't you the book traveller?'

Condor replied that he was and Nisbet said that he had seen him up at Stobswood the previous July. The two men were in conversation all the way to Widdrington.

Along that journey, Condor saw Nisbet excuse himself as the train approached Heaton. He then lowered the window, looked out and had a conversation with a woman.

As the train continued on its way, Condor said that if Nisbet could find new customers for him he would happily pay him half of the commission he earned. Nisbet was excited by the idea and agreed, adding that his present position was not that well paid. As the new partnership was agreed, Condor noticed that the train was at Stannington. He got out at the next station, Morpeth.

On Tuesday, 15 March, Condor returned home to his lodgings at the top of Westgate Road at about 5.30pm to find a letter waiting for him, from his wife. When he read it he learned to his dismay that his wife had fallen into hire purchase debt. There was also money owed for the rent on the cottage and she had been informed by the landlord that if she did not pay £5 by Saturday, 19 March, she would be evicted.

Condor's original idea was to collect as much money as he could from his customers on the Friday and then run home to the cottage and his wife. He soon realised that this wouldn't work. His employer would immediately report the matter to the police and he would eventually be sent to prison. Then he thought of a new idea. He knew that his new friend Nisbet would be carrying around £400 that same Friday.

Condor already had a revolver and three large lead bullets. He also had some smaller nickel-capped bullets and used brown paper to make them fit into the chamber of his gun. (This idea would have been common knowledge after Dickman's trial.)

Condor knew that the longest part of Nisbet's journey was between Stannington and Morpeth: a total of six minutes. It was also the only

Bogus Information and a Confession

place along that line that the train reached full speed and so made more noise.

On Thursday, 17 March, Condor travelled up to Morpeth with a small shovel and his revolver. It was loaded with just two of the paper packed nickel-capped bullets.

He left Morpeth and turned east. He walked about three quarters of a mile and saw no one. Satisfied that he was not being observed he climbed into a field where there was the stump of an old tree. He then used his shovel to dig a cavity beneath the stump. He then covered the hole with clods of turf before hiding the shovel under a hedge close by.

Condor then walked on a further quarter of a mile or so and fired both bullets from his revolver. The paper packing seemed to work fine and, satisfied that all was ready, he walked back to Morpeth and caught a train back to Newcastle. That night he loaded his revolver with three lead bullets and two nickel-plated ones.

The day for the murder had arrived. On Friday, 18 March, Condor entered the ticket office at Newcastle station. There was a queue of about six people at the window. At the very front was Nisbet. After he had received his ticket Nisbet turned to walk away, saw Condor, and nodded to him. He then crossed to the far side of the ticket office and waited for Condor to get his ticket and join him.

As he waited, Condor saw that the man who had been behind Nisbet, a man he now knew to be Dickman, passed close by Nisbet after getting his ticket. The two men exchanged a few words before Dickman walked on towards the platforms. Dickman was wearing a dark brown overcoat.

Condor and Nisbet walked towards the train, along the platform. Condor had intended to get into the very first compartment but as they approached it he saw a young man standing at the window, talking to someone else who was inside the same compartment. He knew he had been seen but noticed that the compartment next to the one where the young man stood, was empty. He invited Nisbet to go into this one. Nisbet agreed and opened the door.

Nisbet sat with his back to the engine. Condor sat facing him. As the train pulled out, Condor handed Nisbet a list of names of potential customers.

At Heaton station, Nisbet stood up, looking for his wife. She was rather breathless when she finally got to the carriage and only had time to exchange a few words with her husband. The train then moved on and the two men settled back into their discussion of the new book selling venture.

At Killingworth station a porter opened the door and shouted down the platform that there was plenty of room there. A stout woman, carrying a large basket and in the company of a girl aged about 15 got in. They finally left at Cramlington.

At Plessey two young men were about to get in but one of them pointed out that it wasn't a smoking compartment and they moved on.

At Stannington, two young men got out of the next compartment and they nodded to Nisbet who nodded back. It was at that station that Nisbet put the list of names inside his coat pocket.

The train gathered speed and Condor pointed out of the window saying, 'What is the name of that colliery where the smoke is rising?' As Nisbet moved forward in his seat and turned his head, Condor fired a bullet into him at close range.

Nisbet fell back into his seat and put both hands up to the side of his head. Seeing the gun for the first time he cried out, 'Good God do you want to murder me?' He then threw himself forward at his attacker.

A second shot was fired but Condor believed it had missed. Nisbet managed to force Condor back onto his seat but then made the mistake of releasing him and making for the carriage doorway. Possibly he intended to pull the communication cord. Unfortunately, he tripped over his assailant's feet, and fell to his knees. Condor then

Bogus Information and a Confession

placed the gun against the base of Nisbet's skull and fired again. He then fired two more shots into Nisbet's still form.

Nisbet lay on the floor, face upwards. Condor opened Nisbet's coat and took back the list of names. He then turned the body over and pushed it underneath the seat. As he did so he accidentally stood on Nisbet's glasses and broke them.

Condor glanced at his watch. He had three minutes before the train reached Morpeth. He wrapped the murder weapon in an old muffler and made a careful examination of his clothing. There appeared to be no obvious stains of blood.

At Morpeth, Condor picked up the bank bag and leapt onto the platform before the train had fully stopped. He saw a man approaching the carriage so hurried on along the platform in case his crime was discovered. He then left the station and, turning east, returned to the tree stump where he had dug the hole.

Once at the stump, Condor cut open the bag and took out just twelve half sovereigns. He then wrapped the muffler around the bag and buried it, along with the gun, in the hole beneath the stump. He then returned to Morpeth and went about his book selling business. It was there, later that day, that he heard the first reports of the murder. He was having a quiet drink in the Newcastle Arms when he heard a railway porter saying that a body had been found at Alnmouth.

Later still, Condor returned to Newcastle where he went to the Post Office and purchased £6 worth of postal orders which he sent on to his wife. The following day, Saturday, 19 March, he read the description given by Percival Hall of the man he had seen with Nisbet at Newcastle. It was a very accurate description of Condor and that gave him some cause for concern.

On Monday, 21 March, Condor received a letter from his wife. She had settled the debts. That same night he read that an arrest had been made.

It was not until Thursday, 21 April, almost a week after the final magistrates' court hearing when Dickman was sent for trial, that

Murder On The Train

Condor returned to his hiding place at the tree stump. He removed all of the gold and silver and took the murder weapon away with him. That evening he dropped the gun into the Tyne, off the Redheugh Bridge.

Sometime around the middle of May, Condor was close to his hiding place when he heard a group of men talking about the problems they were having with water getting into a certain pit. Condor thought that if he dropped the bank bag down this particular shaft it would actually help Dickman. After all, he was in custody and couldn't possibly drop it down there himself. It was either 1 or 2 June when Condor dropped it down there, even adding a piece of cardboard on which he had written in capital letters 'Dickman is innocent'. Unfortunately, when the bag was found a few days later, there was no mention of the cardboard.

Condor's confession had one final barb for the police. He stated that after the guilty verdict and the death sentence, he was on the quayside when he heard a group of men talking about the crime. One of the men said he had travelled on the murder train. He had boarded at Killingworth and got into the first compartment of the last coach. There were six people in the compartment. One of them was a well-dressed man who sat with his back to the engine. He had a heavy black moustache and had placed his overcoat on the rack above his head. He was reading a sporting paper. The man on the quay went on to say that after Dickman had been sent for trial, he went to the Pilgrim Street police station and told the officers what he had seen and that he might be an alibi for Dickman. The superintendent ordered him out of the office and threatened to arrest him if he spread the story.

What are we to make of such a confession? We can say, to begin with, that there are many errors in the narrative. Condor states that Nisbet travelled with his back to the engine and we know that this is not the case. At Heaton station, Cicely Nisbet saw a man sitting in that position. Nisbet, therefore, would have sat facing the engine.

Condor also makes a mistake over the bullets. He claims to have fired three lead bullets and two nickel-capped ones. The evidence of the severity of the wounds indicates that only two lead bullets were fired, along with three nickel-capped.

There must also be disquiet over the description of the murder itself. Logic dictates that the very first shot, or at the very least, one of the first two, was the one to the side of the head in which a lead bullet inflicted a great deal of damage. Nisbet would have been unable to offer any resistance after that and a scenario in which he struggles with his attacker and all but overcomes him is untenable.

Condor states that he chose to commit the crime between Stannington and Morpeth as that was the longest part of the journey. This too is in error. Whilst it is true that the journey time between Stannington and Morpeth is six minutes, that between Heaton and Forest Hall was seven minutes. We must also consider that there would be much less chance of the crime being discovered at Forest Hall than there would be at Morpeth.

The matter of Condor jumping from the train whilst it was still moving also does not hold water. John Grant was waiting for the train at Morpeth, he saw no one in the murder compartment and also did not see anyone leave it. He would certainly have remembered a man leaping from a still moving train and having to slam the door behind him.

These and other factors show that the confession is an invention. It is written by someone who knows a good deal about the case, but has been unable to satisfactorily explain away such anomalies as John Grant not seeing anyone leave the compartment, and the use of two weapons. Why was it written then, and by whom?

Most researchers believe that the Condor confession was penned by Clarence Henry Norman, the court shorthand writer at Dickman's trial.

Norman heard all the evidence at the trial and was convinced that there had been a miscarriage of justice. On 24 July 1910, he wrote to Home Secretary Winston Churchill, with a detailed list of his concerns. He also contacted a friend of his, John Burns, who was a member of the Cabinet, asking him to intercede on Dickman's behalf.

On 6 August 1910, Norman wrote an article for the *Daily News*. It was entitled 'Ought Dickman to be Hanged?' and outlined his concerns and arguments over the verdict. Once the death sentence had been confirmed, Norman wrote to Churchill a second time, all to no avail.

The next few years saw Norman involved in other pursuits. He joined the Independent Labour Party and was active in the campaign against the Great War. He became treasurer of the Stop The War Committee and joined the campaign against the imprisonment of anti-war objectors. As a result of these activities, he was arrested on 27 June 1916. He was in court again on 8 February 1917, accused of persuading other conscientious objectors, who were held at Dartmoor, to refuse to work. Found guilty he was sentenced to a year's hard labour.

Norman was released after the war ended and returned to his work as a shorthand writer. When, in 1949, Clement Atlee set up a Royal Commission to look into the matter of capital punishment, Norman wrote to him about the Dickman case. In that letter he claimed that he had been in communication with Sir Sidney Orme Rowan-Hamilton, the author of *The Trial of John Alexander Dickman*. Norman claimed that, Rowan-Hamilton said that Dickman had also murdered Caroline Luard in 1909. Winston Churchill had been a close friend of Charles Luard, the dead woman's husband, who eventually committed suicide. The implication was that Churchill had assisted in framing Dickman in order to avenge the Luards.

Clarence Henry Norman certainly had an axe to grind over capital punishment in general and the Dickman case in particular and may well have been the man who wrote Condor's confession. It matters not either way. The confession is erroneous in matters of fact and deduction and is certainly not written by the man who fired those bullets into John Nisbet's head.

Chapter 33

If Dickman Were Innocent

It is a simple enough conclusion: if Dickman was an innocent man, then he was telling the truth in his interviews with the police, at the magistrates' court, and at his trial. It also means that his wife, Annie, was also telling the truth when she wrote to the newspapers. What, then, does this imply?

It implies that on the morning of 18 March, whilst Annie was busying herself in the kitchen at around 9.45am, her husband told her that he was going out and if he wasn't back home by about 12.20pm, he would have gone to Stannington.

At about 10.00am, Dickman left home. He was wearing a flannel shirt, with a tie, black boots and a brown overcoat, a pair of brown gloves and a black hat. He caught a tram into Newcastle, getting off at the foot of Northumberland Street and, after originally deciding to walk down to the quay, changed his mind, believing that he didn't have enough time. He walked along Grey Street, cut through High Bridge, and went to the railway station.

He queued up to purchase a return ticket to Stannington and noticed, in front of him, a man he knew by sight, John Innes Nisbet. The two men exchanged a polite 'Good morning' and then Nisbet left the ticket hall, never to be seen again by Dickman.

After buying his ticket, Dickman went to the kiosk and bought himself a *Manchester Sporting Chronicle*. He then went to the third-class refreshment room where he enjoyed a pie and a pint, leaving there at about 10.20am. He then walked through the gate which led to platforms 4 and 5 but turned to his right initially, walked on to platform

8 and used the gentleman's urinal there. He then boarded the 10.27 train, taking a seat towards the rear of the train. The train was just about to leave. Dickman put his overcoat on the rack above his head and began to read the articles about the Grand National, in his newspaper.

People got in and out of Dickman's compartment but, so engrossed was he in his newspaper that he took no real notice of them. He also missed his stop at Stannington, and it was only when the train began to swerve, as it approached Morpeth, that Dickman realised where he was. He quickly grabbed his coat and prepared to leave the train.

Dickman left the station at the south end, taking his ticket out of his waistcoat pocket and handing it to the collector with the excess fare. The ticket collector tore the ticket in two and handed Dickman the return half. Dickman then turned to the west, to walk back towards the Dovecot mine.

Dickman's original intention was to leave the train at Stannington, walk to Dovecot and see Mr Hogg. Once he had finished his business he would then walk to Morpeth, buy a single ticket for Stannington, and catch the express train back to Newcastle. By missing his stop it meant that, in effect, he would do the journey in reverse. He would walk to Dovecot, then back to Stannington station and catch the slow stopping train back to Newcastle.

Unfortunately, somewhere along his route Dickman fell ill. He had long suffered from piles and a sudden attack meant that he had to climb into a field and lie down in the hope that the discomfort would pass. After some time he felt able to walk, albeit slowly, and decided that he would return to Morpeth and catch the express, which left at around 1.10pm.

Such was his discomfort that he arrived at Morpeth too late to catch the express. He knew that the next train was the 1.40pm stopping train so he decided to walk into Morpeth and see if Mr Hogg was in the Newcastle Arms where he sometimes went for lunch. As he approached the bridge he met Elliott and Sanderson and they talked briefly about the big race the next day. He then decided that it would be best, after all, if he went back to the station, which he did.

If Dickman Were Innocent

It should, perhaps, be pointed out that the very fact that Dickman walked on into Morpeth might be held to be proof of his innocence. If he had just shot a man five times, stolen the money, walked to the Isabella shaft, and thrown the bag down there after taking out the money, why would he then take time out to stroll into Morpeth? He would have made certain that he caught the express so that he would be back in Newcastle as quickly as possible.

When he did finally get back to Newcastle, Dickman bought himself a cup of coffee, which seemed to help ease his pain a little more. He finally reached home at around 5.00pm. Annie was entertaining a friend and Dickman invited the lady to stay for tea. She declined. Neither lady noticed anything out of the ordinary in Dickman's behaviour, and there were no obvious signs of blood staining on his clothing.

That evening, Dickman and his wife went to the Pavilion theatre. On the Saturday, Dickman accompanied his wife and daughter into the city centre, to do some shopping. This proved that he could not have travelled back to the Morpeth area on 19 March, to dump the leather bag Nisbet had been carrying.

Dickman's innocence would, of course, also mean that someone else was responsible for the murder of John Innes Nisbet. The most likely scenario, taking in to account what we have already discussed, is that two different calibres of bullet implies two different weapons, which in turn suggests that two killers were responsible.

The suggestion that Dickman was innocent also means that we have a number of questions that must be answered. Amongst these questions are:

1. If Nisbet were alive at Stannington, as evidenced by the testimony of Hall and Spink, and was dead by the time the train reached Morpeth, as shown by the fact that his carriage seemed to be empty, how did the killers escape?
2. Was Nisbet killed by a stranger, or someone he knew?

3. If there were two killers, why was there only one person in the compartment with Nisbet at Heaton station?
4. Why did no one else, apparently, get into the same compartment as Nisbet and his companion between Heaton and Stannington?
5. How are we to explain the identification evidence of Wilson Hepple?
6. Why did Hepple wait until Sunday to make his telephone call to the police?
7. Why and when was the bag placed down the Isabella pit shaft?
8. What is the significance, if any, of the so-called test firing, which splintered the wood on the outside of a carriage on 4 March, precisely two weeks prior to the murder?
9. Why were the police seemingly so intent on having Dickman pay the penalty for this crime, even going so far as to assist in Hall's identification of him as the man he had seen with Nisbet?
10. Does the idea of two killers make at least as much sense as Dickman acting alone?

The answers to these, and other questions, must paint a picture of the events of 18 March, that shows an alternative explanation of the events of that day, which underlines the innocence of Dickman.

We have, largely, demolished the identification evidence, the financial evidence and the firearms evidence. Such evidence of bloodstains that there was, is neither here or there. Insignificant amounts were found, the samples being so small that tests could not even show that it was human.

Circumstantial evidence hanged John Alexander Dickman. That same evidence must show that there is another answer, that fits the known facts even better than did the case presented to the court in July.

Section Three

TWO OTHER MURDERS

Chapter 34

The Murder of Caroline Luard

Before we can proceed to an alternative explanation of the events of 18 March 1910, we need to mention two other brutal killings, both of which remain unsolved to this day. These are the murders of Caroline Luard in 1908 and Herman Cohen in 1909.

Once Dickman had been executed the disquiet about his conviction, the circumstantial evidence and such things as the police subterfuge at the identity parade, continued to cause discussion and debate. It was this which led to suggestions that even if Dickman had been innocent of Nisbet's murder, justice had been done as there was evidence linking him to two other murders. We will see that there is no truth in either accusation.

Caroline Luard was 58 years old in 1909 and lived with her husband, 69 year old Charles Edward Luard, a retired major general at a house named Ightham Knoll, close to the village of Ightham, near Sevenoaks, in Kent. The couple had had two children, both boys. The youngest of these, Eric Dalbiac Luard had died from a fever in 1903 whilst on service with the army in Africa. The eldest son, Charles Elmhirst Luard, born in 1876, was also serving in the army, in South Africa.

The Luards had moved to Ightham Knoll in 1888 and by all accounts were a most devoted couple. They would often go on long walks, taking the family Irish Setter with them, and things were no different on the afternoon of Monday, 24 August 1908.

Caroline Luard had invited a neighbour, Alice Mary Stewart, for afternoon tea, the lady being due to call at around 4.20pm, so she

The Murder of Caroline Luard

knew she would not be able to stay out very long. In fact, it was Charles who really wished to go out, as he wanted to pick his golf clubs up from the Godden Green course, where he had left them. Caroline said she would accompany him on the walk, though. They left their home at 2.30pm.

The couple set out with no particular route planned. They walked for half an hour or so before parting at a wicket gate that led into Fish Pond woods. Charles then took the dog on with him, towards the golf club, whilst Caroline set out through the woods. It was now 3.00pm.

There was a summer house in the woods, known as La Casa. Though it belonged to Mr Horace Wilkinson, he allowed the Luards to use it when they wished, something they often did in their strolls through the wood.

Charles Luard arrived at the golf club, where he was seen by a number of witnesses. He then began the walk home, which would take him an hour or so. Along the way, the Reverend Arthur Benjamin Cotton drove up in his car and offered Luard a lift. He accepted and the general was dropped off at the gates to his house.

When he went inside, General Luard found Mrs Stewart waiting for him. It was now 4.30pm. Luard apologised for the fact that his wife had not been at home to greet Mrs Stewart and said he thought she would be home very soon. They then waited five more minutes before having tea together.

As the minutes passed without any sign of Mrs Luard, the general became rather concerned and said that he believed his wife might have fallen ill and he felt he should go to look for her. Mrs Stewart said that she would accompany him part of the way, but would have to return home as she was expecting a guest of her own.

General Luard and Mrs Stewart walked back towards the woods where he had parted from his wife earlier that day, whilst Mrs Stewart made her own way home. The general walked on into the woods and approached the summer house. As he drew near, he saw his wife lying on the verandah and thought she might have collapsed. It was only as he crouched down close to her that he saw the pool of blood. It was clear that Caroline was dead. General Luard ran for help. The time was now 5.15pm (*see Plates 29 and 30*).

The surgeon and police attended. An initial examination showed that Caroline had received an injury to her head, possibly from a blow, but she had also been shot twice at close range. One of her gloves had been torn from her hand and three valuable rings stolen. A pocket in her dress had also been torn away.

The inquest on the dead woman opened on Saturday, 18 September, in the Luard's dining room, before Mr H. Buss, the Kent county coroner.

Medical evidence was given by Dr Mansfield and Dr Walker, who had performed the post-mortem together. They had found a wound at the back of the head which they originally believed had been caused by a blow from a bludgeon. Later they would suggest that in fact this wound had been caused when Caroline fell to the floor after the first shot had been fired.

Two bullets were extracted from Caroline's head. One from behind the right ear, and the other from underneath the left eye. The bullets were of small calibre. After this medical evidence had been given, the proceedings were adjourned for two weeks.

The funeral of the victim took place on Friday, 28 August, by which time Scotland Yard had been called in to assist the Kent police. Detective Chief Inspector Scott and Detective Sergeant Percy Savage travelled to the county from London.

In a case of murder such as this, the surviving spouse is usually initially regarded as a suspect. General Luard, however, was quickly eliminated from the enquiry. Thomas Durrant, a manager to Mr Bligh, a brewer of Sevenoaks, had seen General Luard at the top of a hill near Hall Farm at 3.30pm. Another witness, Ernest King, a labourer, was working on the golf links and saw General Luard at some time around 3.25pm. Henry King, the steward at the Godden Golf Club saw the general walking across the greens at 3.30pm. All of these sightings showed that the general could not be the man who fired the shots that killed Caroline Luard as he was too far from the woods at the time the murder took place.

It had been easy to determine the precise time of the attack upon Mrs Luard. Two witnesses, Annie Wickham and Daniel Kettel both reported hearing shots at 3.15pm, by which time Charles Luard was more than a mile away from the woods.

The inquest reopened on 9 September, at the George and Dragon hotel in Ightham. In addition to the witnesses already mentioned, Edwin John Churchill, a firearms expert, was called to give his testimony on the bullets used to kill Mrs Luard. Both of the bullets recovered were .320 calibre. General Luard owned two revolvers but both were of .450 calibre and could not have been the murder weapon.

A verdict of murder by person or persons unknown was returned but this was not the end of the matter. General Luard began to receive anonymous letters accusing him of being the murderer. One after another came to his home, and so distressed did he become, that Colonel Warde, the brother of the chief constable of the county invited Luard to stay with him at his country estate, Barham Court, near Maidstone. Meanwhile, Luard's surviving son had been informed of his mother's death and boarded a ship bounds for Southampton. His ship was due to dock on 18 September.

General Luard fell into a deeper and deeper depression and, the day before his son was due to arrive in England, he took no breakfast but sat down to write a letter. Later he walked out of Barham Court, to the local railway line, and threw himself under a speeding train. Pinned to his body was a note: 'Whoever finds me take me to Colonel Warde.'

Back in his room at Barham Court, Warde found the last letter Luard had written that morning. It began,

> My dear Warde,
> I am sorry to have to return your kindness and long friendship in this way, but I am satisfied that it is best to

join her in the second life at once, as I can be of no further use to anyone in this world, of which I am tired and in which I do not wish to live any longer.

I thought that my strength was sufficient to bear up against the horrible imputations and terrible letters, which I have received since that awful crime was committed and which robbed me of my happiness. And so it was for a time, and the goodness, kindness and sympathy of so many friends kept me going.

But somehow in the last day or two, something seems to have snapped. The strength has left me and I care for nothing except to join her again. So goodbye my dear friend, to both of us.

Yours very affectionately,
C.E. Luard.

P.S. I shall be somewhere on the railway line.

The murder of Caroline Luard was never solved. The original police thought was that an itinerant had come upon Mrs Luard in the summer house and murdered her for her rings and the contents of her pocket. The more the investigation proceeded, the more that train of thought appeared untenable.

Such an opportunist thief would have been unlikely to have been carrying a revolver on the off chance that he might find a suitable victim. No strangers had been reported in the area. None of the rather distinctive jewellery was ever traced, despite detailed descriptions being circulated around the entire country. As the inquiry ground to a halt, police thinking was that the killer had known Mrs Luard, that the crime was planned and that the theft of the rings from her hand was nothing more than an attempt to mislead investigators about the motive for the crime.

How, then, does the name of John Alexander Dickman come into this case. The original source for the suggestion is

The Murder of Caroline Luard

Sir Sidney Orme Rowan-Hamilton who wrote *The Trial of John Alexander Dickman*, one of the volumes in the famous trial series. He claimed that Mrs Luard had responded to an advertisement that Dickman had placed in *The Times*, asking for financial help. She had sent him a small cheque, but he had then altered the amount, changing the tens figure into hundreds. When Caroline discovered the subterfuge she wrote to Dickman and arranged a meeting, without her husband's knowledge. Rather than either pay the money back, or risk going to jail for fraud, he had shot her to death.

This suggestion is full of holes. On the day of the murder, the Luards had no planned route for their walk, so Caroline could hardly have made an appointment to meet someone at the summer house in the woods. Dickman was a stranger to the area and, as noted above, no strangers were reportedly seen in the area.

It is, however, Dickman's own trial for murder which is the best indicator of his innocence. Caroline Luard was murdered on 24 August 1908. If there was any truth in the story of the altered cheque then the transaction must have taken place in the summer of that same year. There would be, then, a transaction in one of his accounts in June or July of 1908.

Dickman had two bank accounts. The first was at the National Provincial Bank in Moseley Street. Details of the transactions from December 1907 onwards were given at the trial. There was no reference to a cheque from Mrs Luard.

The second account was with Lloyds Bank and details of the transaction from 31 December 1907, were listed. Again there was no mention of a cheque from Mrs Luard.

Dickman had been charged with a murder in which all the evidence was circumstantial. There was a reasonable chance that he might be found innocent. Had the police found, in their examination of Dickman's bank accounts, that there had been a cheque paid in from Caroline Luard's account, and that this cheque had been altered by

Dickman, there would have been a direct link of concrete evidence between Dickman and the murder in Kent.

Dickman was never charged with the murder of Caroline Luard, nor was he even questioned about it. The idea that he was somehow involved in her murder is nothing but pure invention in an attempt to sully the name of a dead man, and persuade a disquiet public that, one way or another, justice had been done.

Chapter 35

The Murder of Herman Cohen

Herman Cohen, a Jewish money-lender, operated his business from the front room of 24 Harold Street, Sunderland, where he lodged with his cousin, Etty Yamkelowitz and her husband, Solomon. Carrying out most of his business during the evenings, Herman would sometimes also sell his customers items from Solomon's drapery business (*see Plate 31*).

On Monday, 8 March 1909, Herman carried on his business as usual. At 6.45pm he popped his head around the door of the kitchen where Solomon and Etty were enjoying a cup of coffee and asked for some shirts for a customer. Solomon was happy to oblige and, after he had handed over the shirts, saw the customer talking to Herman as he was about to leave. Solomon also saw a tall man at the foot of the stairs, waiting to see Herman. Knowing that Herman valued his privacy when dealing with customers, Solomon returned to the kitchen.

Some fifteen minutes or so later, the front doorbell rang. Whenever anyone called at this hour it was usually someone wishing to do business with Herman, so Soloman and Etty ignored it. Besides, the front door was always left unlocked when Herman was seeing customers so, sooner or later whoever it was would try the door and find that it was open. It was not until the bell had rung two or three times that Solomon said, 'Would you get that dear? Herman must have stepped out for a minute.'

Etty put down the book she was reading and went to the door. As she passed the front room she glanced inside and saw that it appeared to be empty. Etty opened the door to find one of Herman's customers, Mrs June Robinson, who wished to pay the 4s she owed as her latest payment. Etty pointed out that Herman didn't seem to be at home, but took the money and gave June a receipt.

Etty Yamkelowitz returned to the kitchen and finished her coffee. She then stood and informed her husband that she was going to see if Herman had come back in yet. She went into the front room, but was back, ashen faced and hysterical, within seconds crying, 'Jacob's lying in the front room.'

Jacob was Solomon's brother and was subject to fits. He didn't live at Harold Street any longer and had lodgings of his own, but he had called earlier that evening. Etty seemed to forget that Jacob had left a couple of hours earlier and that she and Solomon had seen him go out of the back door.

Solomon went into the front room, accompanied by his wife. The room was dimly lit, but there was the clear shape of a figure lying on the floor in a pool of blood. Only now did Solomon notice that the prostrate figure was wearing slippers. It wasn't his brother Jacob, but his lodger Herman Cohen.

Though he was very badly injured, Herman was still alive. As Solomon cradled his head, Herman opened his eyes briefly and gave out a low moan. It was clear that he was in need of urgent medical attention.

Solomon ran for help, calling first at the house of Mr Bergson across the road and asking him to go to the aid of his wife. He then ran on to fetch the doctor.

Doctor Beveridge arrived at the house at 7.30pm by which time the place seemed to be filled with relatives, friends and neighbours, all of whom had heard about the event and come to see what assistance they could offer. Beveridge noted that Herman had received some very severe head injuries and his brain was exposed in places. Soon afterwards, a second medical gentleman, Dr Gordon Bell arrived but despite the ministrations of two doctors,

The Murder of Herman Cohen

Herman Cohen died from his injuries at around 7.50pm. He had never regained consciousness.

The police began their investigation, led by Superintendent Hately. He began by ordering a thorough search of all the yards and gardens in the vicinity, hoping that his men would find a murder weapon. They found nothing.

The gentleman who had purchased the shirts from Herman was traced. He was able to account for his movements after he had left the house, but was also able to tell the officers about the tall man, wearing a light coloured overcoat, who had been waiting in the lobby to see Herman.

The investigation was stepped up. Cohen's books were examined and every client traced and interviewed. Rumours began to abound in the area and there were reports that a man had been seen putting something down a drain on the night of the murder. Every drain in the area was lifted and searched but again the police found nothing.

A publican from the east end of town came forward to say that his staff had served a tall man wearing a light coloured overcoat, on the night of the murder. He spoke with a foreign accent and one of the barmaids saw that he had blood on his hands. He left the pub after quickly drinking a glass of beer. Despite a massive police effort, the tall man was never traced.

At the inquest, Dr Beveridge reported that when he attended the scene, he had found Mr Cohen lying in a large pool of blood. There were two pieces of his skull bone in that pool. Dr Beveridge noted eight wounds in all, one of which was so severe that a piece of Herman's skull had been sliced off and was only attached to his head by a piece of scalp. The weapon used to inflict the injuries was most probably an axe, but could have been something like a butcher's cleaver. In addition to the massive head injuries, Herman's little finger had been almost severed from one hand, possibly when he tried to protect himself from the onslaught. The position of the wounds indicated that Mr Herman had initially been attacked from behind, whilst he was seated at his desk.

There could be no other verdict but murder by person or persons unknown. The killer of Herman Cohen was never found. How, then, was Dickman's name put forward as a possible suspect?

The responsibility belongs to an article in *The People* newspaper of 14 August 1910, published less than a week after Dickman had been hanged. In that article, the author claimed that when Dickman had been searched, the police had found the diamond ring that Cohen wore on the finger which had been severed in the attack. He also had on him a £5 note, taken from Cohen at the time of the robbery. Finally, so certain were the police of Dickman's guilt that they were present at the appeal court to arrest him for Cohen's murder, should he be successful in having his conviction quashed.

Once again the article is full of inaccuracies. To begin with, Herman Cohen's finger was not actually severed. It was attached by a flap of skin and only fell off during the doctor's attempts to save his life. It was then placed on Cohen's desk still wearing the supposedly stolen ring.

The crime took place in March 1909. Dickman was not arrested for Nisbet's murder until one year later. The authorities claimed that his motive for the crime was financial desperation and yet he is supposed to have kept a £5 note for a full year without using it. There is also the fact that only 20 or 30s in cash was actually stolen from Cohen's office.

Turning to the planned arrest at the appeal, the police would have found it very difficult to carry out their plan. The appeal was heard in London and Dickman chose not to attend. At the time the appeal was heard, Dickman was still in his cell at Newcastle.

The final point is that the killer of Herman Cohen, whoever he was, must have been covered in blood. He would also have had to carry with him the bloodstained weapon he had used. If Dickman were the killer then he had to walk through the streets of Sunderland, probably return to the railway station, catch a train back to Newcastle, then probably a tram back to Lily Avenue and all without being noticed.

The Murder of Herman Cohen

There was not a shred of evidence linking Dickman to this crime. It was merely an attempt, by the newspaper, to increase their circulation by printing untruths about a man no longer able to defend himself.

The truth is that Herman Cohen was probably murdered by someone who lived in the vicinity of Harold Street and, whoever that person was, it most certainly was not John Alexander Dickman.

Section Four

AN ALTERNATE SOLUTION

Chapter 36

A Review

One of the strongest tenets of the circumstantial evidence against Dickman was the identification evidence. Whilst John Spink's amounted to very little, and that of Percival Hall can be discredited, we are left with two witnesses who say they saw Dickman at Newcastle station, in the company of Nisbet – Charles Raven and Wilson Hepple. For the sake of completeness, we will use some of Hall's testimony to see if it agrees with the other two.

No one ever bothered to ask what time Nisbet left his office with the pay cheque, what time he arrived at Lloyds Bank, and what time he left that bank. We cannot, therefore, determine what time he would have arrived at the station, or what time he purchased his ticket. What times can we actually deduce?

Charles Raven said that he was at the station at around 10.20am. He was walking along the concourse, towards the gateway to platforms 4 and 5, so that the first-class and third-class refreshment rooms were on his left (*see Plate 17*).

Raven was walking into the scene on Plate 17. Where we are looking is his direction of travel. He will have passed the large clock and may not have noticed the precise time but, it is safe to assume that he wouldn't be far out in his estimate of the time. What then of the evidence of Wilson Hepple?

Hepple said that he arrived at the station at around 10.07am and went directly to the booking hall. It was some considerable time before the ticket window opened and Hepple was the second person to purchase a ticket. It was whilst he was in the booking hall that he

A Review

saw Dickman, a man he had known for many years, but whom he then did not bother to speak to, even to say 'Good morning.'

After this, Hepple went onto the concourse to see which platform the train was due to depart from. Once again he had to wait some time before the board was put up. He then went directly to the train, chose his compartment and placed his parcels onto the rack. It was then that he decided to pace up and down, on the platform.

At Dickman's trial, Hepple said that he had been pacing up and down the platform, for seven or eight minutes before there were signs that the train was about to leave. Assuming the smaller of those two times, Hepple started his pacing at around 10.20am. In summary, his basic evidence therefore dictates that Hepple was at the station at 10.07am, and began his pacing at 10.20am. That gives him thirteen minutes, which would be swallowed up by his waiting, buying a ticket, waiting on the concourse and then walking to the train.

Although Hall's later identification at the police line-up is unsatisfactory, he said that Nisbet and his companion got onto the train just as it was about to leave. Once again we will err on the side of caution and say that this was at about 10.26am.

Do these timings all confirm each other? Raven said he saw Dickman and Nisbet pass through the gates to the platform at around 10.20am. This was about the same time that Hepple said he began his pacing, but both he and Hall say that the two men got onto the train at about 10.26am, meaning that they had a six minute walk to get to the compartment where the murder took place. At a normal walking pace, that would equate to a distance of some 350 yards.

Of course people could be mistaken. Perhaps Raven saw the two men four or five minutes later, but this shows that one should not simply accept such evidence as perfectly accurate and use it to draw a time line of events.

We have already asked why did Hepple not at least pass the time of day with someone he knew so well? He had purchased his own ticket, turned to leave and saw Dickman. What could be easier than just passing down the queue and speaking to him?

There are other questions that need to be considered. Hepple said he was pacing up and down outside his compartment. Hall said he was looking out of the window of his compartment and saw Dickman and Nisbet walking towards him. At the same time, Hepple was watching the two men, as he paced. Why then, at no stage, did Hall ever refer to seeing a man pacing up and down the platform? He could have mentioned him, possibly given a description of him, so that the police might appeal to him to come forward as a witness.

Yet another question relates to both Hall and Spink. They were never asked what time they had arrived at the station, when they had purchased their tickets, or when they got on to the train. Hepple's testimony shows that as soon as the platform was announced, he went and selected his carriage. Did he not see Hall and Spink pass him and take their own compartment close to the engine? Did he not see Hall looking out of the window? Did he not notice either of them at Stannington as the train pulled out? Remember they had to wait until the entire train had pulled out so they could cross the line and walk on to the Netherton colliery.

Perhaps what these witnesses didn't say should be viewed to be as important as what they did say.

Another question is the time of the train itself. In the first newspaper reports, Hepple said he caught the 10.29am train, but we know that the train left Newcastle at 10.27am. It might be argued that this was a simple typographical error in the newspaper reports, in which case it should be pointed out that two different newspapers made the same 'typographical' error.

Hepple had a studio at 7 Gallowgate. If he walked from there to catch the train back to his home then he could have walked to either the Central station or the Manors. Both were about the same distance from Gallowgate. He had, however, been shopping as he carried parcels with him. Surely that shopping would have taken place in the city centre, which is closer to Manors station. Curiously, the train left the Manors station at 10.29am. Does this indicate that Hepple was never actually at Newcastle Central? Could it be that Hepple actually caught the train at the Manors, and as he looked for a seat he saw Dickman reading his newspaper? If so, what possible reason could he have had for lying?

Some writers have suggested that it is a telling point that Hepple only came forward after the newspapers had published details of a reward of £100. Perhaps a little embellishment so that his testimony would agree with that of Hall's, details of which had already been printed in the newspapers.

A piece of circumstantial evidence that was never used at the trial, but was suggested in the newspapers, was the test firing of a weapon exactly two weeks before the murder, that is Friday, 4 March.

Mr A.G. Brocklehurst was travelling from Newcastle to Morpeth when he and the other passengers in his compartment were startled by what sounded like a shot. Upon looking out Brocklehurst saw that the wooden frame of the carriage door was splintered, apparently by a bullet or bullets fired from another carriage. Brocklehurst was travelling in the last compartment of the second carriage from the engine, and the shot was fired somewhere between Annitsford and Stannington. This has been used to suggest that Dickman were testing one of his guns, to see if the shot could be heard.

The train on which Brocklehurst was travelling was an express, and the first stop was Morpeth. The 1910 railway timetable shows that this train left Newcastle at 9.35am, and would have arrived at Morpeth at 9.59am.

The evidence of the surveyor Charles Franklin Murphy, one of the early witnesses at Dickman's trial, shows that the distance from Stannington station to the Dovecot mine was one and three eights of a mile. He also stated that the distance from Morpeth station to Dovecot was three and three quarter miles. Finally, we have the evidence of

William Hogg who said that Dickman did visit him on 4 March, and that he arrived at about noon.

We know that Dickman visited Dovecot on 4 March, but which train did he catch? He said he caught the 10.27am stopping train again, but the practice shooting scenario means he would have had to have caught the 9.35am express.

If he caught the 10.27am, he would have arrived at Stannington at 11.06am and had a one and three eights of a mile walk to do in about an hour. If he caught the 9.35am, he would have arrived at Morpeth at 9.59am and would have had about two hours to do a three and three quarter mile walk.

Both journeys are possible and this does indicate that Dickman could have been the person who fired a shot on 4 March, but it also shows that *anyone*, travelling on that train, possibly someone who had to journey back to the Stannington area, whether to visit the Dovecot mine or to go to the region of the Isabella pit shaft, could have tested a gun.

In 1910, circumstantial evidence convicted John Alexander Dickman of murder. It is now time to show that the same kind of evidence could build a case, at least as strong, against someone else.

Chapter 37

The Murder of John Innes Nisbet

In *The Sign of Four* published in 1890, Sherlock Holmes remarks, 'How often have I said to you that when you have eliminated the impossible, whatever remains, however improbable, must be the truth?'

Despite all the rhetoric about financial problems, the possession of guns, weak alibis and witness identifications, there is one fundamental tenet in the murder of John Innes Nisbet that is the foundation stone of the entire case.

According to the evidence given against Dickman, the testimony of the various witnesses shows that Nisbet was alive at Stannington station and his carriage was apparently empty at Morpeth. He must, therefore, have been killed between those two stations and we know, indisputably, that Dickman got off the train at Morpeth.

We are, however, faced with a major problem. John Grant, who was waiting for the train at Morpeth, did not see anyone get out of the compartment where the murder took place, and looked into the compartment as he passed it, seeing that no one was there. He would have travelled in that compartment if it hadn't been a non-smoking one. So, if Dickman were the killer, how can we explain this anomaly? Dickman must have killed Nisbet between Stannington and Morpeth, got off the train at Morpeth, but did not, apparently, get out of the carriage where the body lay beneath the seat.

If it could have been proved that Nisbet was alive at Morpeth and was, instead, murdered somewhere between that station and his intended stop, Widdrington, then Dickman must have been innocent.

He was no longer on the train after Morpeth. There have been writers who tried to suggest that this was the case, but their arguments rely on supposition and guesswork. There is, however, an alternate explanation, and one that has never been explored in any other book. The only other possible explanation, if Dickman was innocent, is that Nisbet was murdered *before* the train pulled in to Stannington.

This, of course, raises a new question of its own. If Nisbet had been shot before Stannington, how did John William Spink and Percival Harding Hall manage to see him alive and well and nod to him? The answer is that they didn't, and the reason for that is very simple indeed: **Percival Harding Hall and John William Spink murdered John Innes Nisbet, somewhere between Heaton and Stannington.**

We have said, many times throughout this book, that the evidence against Dickman was purely circumstantial. Let us now look at the supposition that Hall and Spink were guilty and see what circumstantial evidence we can present against them.

To begin with, we can determine who was sitting where during the early part of the journey from Newcastle. At Heaton station, Cicely Nisbet saw her husband and noted that there was someone else sitting in his compartment. That someone was sitting on the far side of the carriage, with his back to the engine. She also saw a young man in the next compartment, standing at the window and looking out. Other testimony showed that this young man was Hall.

This has always appeared curious. Hall stated in his evidence that he had been looking out of the carriage window at Newcastle and again at Heaton. Why should he do this? He had been making the same journey for years. Surely it would have become a matter of pure routine for him yet, on this particular day he seemed to spend most of his time, at least as far as Heaton, standing up and gazing out of the open window. Could he have simply been watching to see who was getting on and off, and hoping, by his presence, to discourage anyone from coming to that particular carriage? Be that as it may, it is clear that Hall, at least at this stage, was travelling in the compartment next

The Murder of John Innes Nisbet

to Nisbet. This means, of course, that it must have been Spink who was travelling with Nisbet, and so it was Spink that Cicely Nisbet saw in the shadows at Heaton.

This leads us to solve a minor mystery in the case. Whoever killed Nisbet would have known of his routine. They would have been aware that Nisbet's wife waited for him at Heaton. At the trial, the suggestion was that Dickman had cajoled Nisbet into travelling at the top end of the train. This served two purposes. First, Cicely Nisbet would have less time to talk to her husband and the sound of the engine would drown out the sound of the shots.

However, if we look at Hall's testimony, he states that it was Nisbet, not his companion, who chose that particular carriage. This cannot have been the case, for the killer must have known that the shadow from the bridge at Heaton would only be cast over certain compartments. It would have been him, not Nisbet, who chose the murder compartment. Hall must have been lying about who made the decision and he lied because it was his partner, Spink, who made it.

The evidence of Cicely Nisbet indicates that as the train left Heaton station, Spink would have been in the same compartment as her husband, sitting directly opposite to him, with his back to the engine. There are five stops between Heaton and Stannington. These stations were Forest Hall, Killingworth, Annitsford, Cramlington and Plessey. The total journey time from leaving Heaton to arriving at Stannington was thirty two minutes.

If Hall left his compartment at the next station, Forest Hall, and climbed in with Nisbet and Spink, then the three men would have been together from 10.41am. This is entirely possible, but Hall may well have entered the murder compartment later. If we recall Mr Brockelbank's story of the shot being fired on 4 March, he stated that this occurred somewhere between Annitsford and Stannington.

How can we possibly narrow this down a little further? Why would Mr Brocklehurst not know precisely when the shot was fired? The answer is simple. Mr Brocklehurst was taking no particular notice as the train made its way north. It was the sound of a shot and the splintering of the wood outside his carriage which woke him from his reverie. Annitsford may have been the last station he actually noticed and, after the shot was fired, Stannington was the next station he recalled. The indication, therefore, is that it is likely the shot was fired between Plessey, the stop before Stannington, and Stannington itself.

If this supposition is accurate, then Hall and Spink planned to murder Nisbet between those two stations. This means that Hall would, almost certainly, have joined Spink and Nisbet at Plessey. This in turn would mean that Hall, perhaps constantly looking out of his open window, would have seen that nobody else would get into either of the two crucial compartments. When the train reached Plessey, Hall knew that the plan was still in operation and his joining Spink, signalled that they should continue with their plot to murder Nisbet and steal the money he was carrying.

When Hall entered the murder compartment, he was greeted by Nisbet. We know this because when Nisbet's body was found, he had only one glove on. A man might travel wearing a pair of gloves or no gloves, but he would be unlikely to travel wearing just one. Much more likely is the suggestion that, as someone he knew by sight entered the compartment, he would stand or at least sit forward, take off the glove on his preferred hand, and shake the hand of the acquaintance.

Wherever he got into the compartment, Hall may have shaken Nisbet's hand and would then have sat down to Nisbet's left, facing the engine. Nisbet was seated on the far right of the compartment, away from the platform side of the train. Since Nisbet did not have time to put his glove back on, the attack would have taken place almost as soon as Hall entered the compartment.

The suggestion of two attackers immediately reduces all the arguments over two guns to nothing. There were two assailants so, naturally, there were two guns. Further, we can even deduce which man had which gun.

We have said that Spink must have been the man with Nisbet at Heaton and he was sitting directly opposite. Hall would then have sat to Nisbet's left. Earlier in this book we discussed the evidence of the wounds inflicted on Nisbet and we saw that the two lead bullets were fired from the left. One of the nickel-plated bullets was fired directly into Nisbet's face. The argument is, therefore, that Hall initially fired from the left and Spink initially fired from the front. This indicates that Hall carried the revolver firing lead bullets whilst Spink carried the automatic pistol, firing nickel-plated bullets.

The wounds indicate that of the five injuries noted, one was from the right, one from in front and three from the left. The logical deduction is that Hall and Spink fired their first shots at the same time. Hall fired a lead bullet from the left and Spink fired a nickel-plated bullet from the front. Nisbet would have fallen back into his seat and to his right, the force of the shot from Hall's revolver possibly twisting his head a little to the right. Both attackers then fired again with both bullets striking Nisbet from the left. Finally, at some stage, possibly after Nisbet had been dragged to the floor and was lying on his left side, Spink fired once more, striking Nisbet close to his right ear. The body was then turned over, possibly in a search for the key to the bank bag, and was then shoved underneath the seat facing the engine.

Such an attack would take no more than a minute or so. This reinforces the suggestion that the most likely place for the shooting was between Stannington and the previous station. Hall and Spink knew that very few people ever got on at Stannington, and the train didn't stay there for very long. That implies that Nisbet was murdered between Plessey and Stannington, which gave Hall and Spink a total of six minutes to kill Nisbet, look for the key, stuff his body underneath the seat and steal the bag.

At Stannington station, the two men left the train and stood outside the compartment where they had just shot a man five times. This was overkill. They had to be absolutely sure that Nisbet was dead as he would have been able to identify them had he survived. Perhaps one of them noticed a man, Andrew Bruce, sitting in the first compartment. If so, all they had to do was nod to an empty compartment, as if they were nodding to Nisbet, thus showing that he was still alive and reinforcing the idea that they had been travelling in the next compartment. When they were interviewed later, as they surely would be, it would also prove that nothing could have occurred before Stannington as they would surely have heard shots coming from the next compartment.

There was a good chance that the body would be found at Morpeth. It was a busy station and the train stayed there for four minutes to take on water. What would Hall and Spink have done had the body been discovered? The answer was quite simple. They had nodded to Nisbet who was alive and well at Stannington, and there was another man with him in the compartment. The implication would be precisely what the police originally thought: that the killer had escaped by jumping from the train somewhere after Stannington.

The two killers then continued on their normal journey towards the Netherton colliery. They probably hid the bank bag and the two guns they had used, somewhere along the road. Even today the roads there are very quiet and there are lots of fields and hedgerows. In 1910, there must have been a hundred likely hiding places. Hall and Spink then delivered their own wage bags and started the walk back to Stannington station and home. During that return journey they could have retrieved the bag, cut it open and removed the gold and silver. They could also have recovered the two guns they had used, at the same time. The area in question was never searched as, during the early stages of the investigation, the police concentrated their efforts along the railway line.

Later that same day, the early reports of the crime showed that the body had not been found until the train reached Alnmouth. This was perfect. Hall and Spink could come forward and describe a man they had seen with Nisbet. That description had to be fairly vague and the one finally published fitted thousands of men in and around Newcastle. Now all the police could determine was that Nisbet must have been murdered between Stannington and Widdrington, where Nisbet would have left the train, had he still been alive.

That was the state of affairs on 18 and 19 March. The evidence the police had at this time indicated that Nisbet was alive at Stannington, there had been a companion at Newcastle, Heaton and Stannington, the crime had probably occurred between Stannington and Widdrington, and two guns had been used, suggesting two killers.

What if there was no arrest? Hall and Spink knew who the killers were, but if the investigation dragged on, without a viable suspect, then sooner or later the fact that there were two killers suggested by the use of two weapons, might have caused them to come under more careful police scrutiny. Then, something happened which helped protect them: Wilson Hepple came forward to put Dickman's name into the frame.

Here we have three possibilities. Hepple may have come forward and given his evidence in good faith. He may, as we suggested earlier, have come forward for the reward. Alternatively, he may even have been cajoled into doing so by one or both of the real killers.

If Hepple acted in good faith, then he described something he believed he had seen. He did say, when giving his evidence, that he saw Dickman in the ticket queue but did not speak to him. That of itself is curious. One would have expected him to speak to a man he knew well but, putting that to one side, his evidence on timings does not agree with that of Charles Raven. One or both must be in error. It might be that Raven saw Nisbet and Dickman apparently walking together through the gateway later than he said, but if his timing was accurate then Hepple could not have seen them together at around 10.26am. More likely is that Hepple saw Dickman in the queue, later saw Nisbet with a companion who had a resemblance to Dickman and confused the two. That is at least as likely as Dickman walking past a man who he must have seen, and who had known him for twenty years, in the company of another man whom he intended to murder within the hour.

We have also said that Hepple may not even have caught the train at Newcastle Central. Whilst it is true that he had a studio in Gallowgate, he stated in his evidence that he had a number of parcels on the day in question. That implies that he had been shopping and the main shopping thoroughfares were around Northumberland Street. The Manors station was positioned much closer to that area than Newcastle Central, and the train did arrive there at 10.29am, which matches the original newspaper reports of what Hepple had said. Did he get on the train there after all? (*see Plate 32*).

If Hepple came forward to collect the reward of £100 then he might simply be describing a man he knew, who he had seen on the train at Manors. This might well explain why he only came forward on the Sunday instead of taking his information to the police at the first opportunity.

What if Hepple was not acting in good faith? How could he possibly have been persuaded to lie about what he had seen by Hall or Spink? The answer may lie in a little family research.

When discussing the identification evidence in Chapter 26 we mentioned that John William Spink was the son of John Kitson Spink and his wife, Mary Ann. Research shows that Mary Ann's maiden name was Heppel. The spelling is not that important. We have seen how officials constantly made errors with John Innes Nisbet's name. Was Spink a relative of Wilson Hepple and was the latter persuaded to lie on his behalf? It may be unlikely but that may also explain why Hepple did not come forward until Sunday.

Whether Hepple was lying, came forward for the reward, or was acting in good faith and mistaken about what he saw, was largely irrelevant. If all that remained of the prosecution evidence was this one identification, then it would not be enough to hang Dickman. It is time to return to the suggestion that Hall and Spink were the murderers.

The Murder of John Innes Nisbet

After Dickman's arrest, the two killers felt themselves safe. At the identification parade Spink could offer no evidence as to Dickman being the killer and Hall made a very tentative one. This was not due to incompetence, or police interference or uncertainty. Hall knew that Dickman was not the killer and had no reason to wish to see an innocent man hang. He deliberately fudged his identification in the belief that either the case would be thrown out at the magistrates' court or, if Dickman were sent for trial, he would be found not guilty. After all, there was no concrete evidence against the man. Surely a jury would be unable to return a guilty verdict on what little evidence there was.

The proceedings continued and Cicely Nisbet made her outburst saying that she now recognised Dickman as the man she had seen at Heaton. Dickman was sent for trial. At some stage after 15 April, the date of the final magistrates' hearing, Hall and Spink changed their minds.

Previously all they had wanted was for someone else to be a suspect. Now that they had seen the evidence, such as it was, it was clear that Dickman was the perfect scapegoat. The circumstantial evidence showed that he had missed his stop on the train, he had no alibi, he had financial problems, there was what appeared to be decent identification evidence from Hepple and Cicely Nisbet, Hall himself had made a tentative identification and there were even suggestions of bloodstains and the purchase of a gun. If only one more piece of evidence could point to Dickman's guilt.

It was that idea which led to the disposal of the bank bag down the Isabella shaft. Hall and Spink waited for a little time after 15 April but at some time between Wednesday, 18 May when the shaft was last inspected, and 9 June, when it was finally found, they dumped the bag down the shaft. Can we possibly determine exactly when the bag was actually put down that shaft?

We know that Hall and Spink made the wages journey on alternate Fridays, and that they made it on 18 March. They would also have made the journey on 1 April, 15 April, 29 April, 13 May, and 27 May. Their next journey would have been on 10 June, by which time the bag had been found. Peter Spooner inspected the shaft on 18 May and found nothing. This leaves us with just one possible date between the previous inspection and the finding of the bag. The most likely date that the bag was dumped down the shaft was Friday, 27 May, meaning that it was only down there for some thirteen days before being discovered.

This immediately accounts for a number of problems. It explains why the bag and the copper coins were not found on two previous shaft inspections. It explains how the bag might have been dumped whilst Dickman was in prison. It also explains why the Isabella shaft was chosen. Dickman might have known that the shaft was subject to flooding and was unused, but Hall and Spink certainly would have. They walked very close to the shaft on their fortnightly wages trips from Stannington station to the Netherton colliery. Indeed, the detour from their normal route to the Isabella shaft would have taken around half an hour or so.

There is, of course, another possibility. It may just have been that by this time Hall and Spink felt that they had nothing more to worry about and just dumped the bag down a shaft where they believed it would never be found. This is unlikely, though, as they would probably know that such shafts were subject to regular inspections.

Whatever the reason, the finding of the bag was a godsend for the prosecution. Now the missing time in Dickman's alibi could be accounted for. Now he hadn't walked along the road to the west and fallen ill. Now he had taken the road to the east of Morpeth station, and walked to the Isabella shaft. It was the final strand in a web of circumstantial evidence and it went a long way towards hanging Dickman.

This suggestion, that Hall and Spink were the killers, is a case at least as strong against that given in court against Dickman. In court a man is innocent until proven guilty. The trial did not prove Dickman guilty. There was certainly a reasonable doubt and this new approach, surmising that Nisbet was murdered before Stannington, and that Hall and Spink were the killers, is a case at least as strong as that outlined against Dickman.

If this scenario could have been presented to the jury in 1910, there is little doubt that John Alexander Dickman would have been found not guilty. As it was, four of the jurymen stated, before Dickman was executed, that if they had known about the police interference and the fact that Cicely Nisbet had known Dickman by sight for eighteen years, they would have found the prisoner not guilty. How many more might have given the same verdict if they had known of these possibilities?

The case against Dickman was weak and circumstantial. His guilt was not proven and he should never have been executed. It is time that the case was reopened with a view to overturning that conviction and sentence.

Chapter 38

Justice

A case at least as strong, if not stronger, than the one presented against Dickman, has been outlined against Hall and Spink. The suggestion that they were the killers solves a number of questions which have remained unanswered for over one hundred years.

In Chapter 33, a number of questions were outlined. How have we answered them?

The first question was, how had the killer escaped? The answer was simple. We no longer have to explain how Nisbet can have been alive at Stannington, dead at Morpeth and yet his murderer did not apparently leave that compartment. Nisbet was dead by the time the train pulled out of Stannington and his killers escaped by nodding to an empty compartment and simply walking away.

The second question was, did Nisbet know his murderer? The man was shot in the head five times. Whoever the attacker was, he was determined that Nisbet must not survive. A stranger need not have done so. The sheer overkill suggests that Nisbet did know his killer and many have said that this is evidence against Dickman. It is equally strong evidence against Hall and Spink who had made the same journey on alternate Fridays for many years. Nisbet knew them better than he knew Dickman. There is even some evidence that Hall and Spink knew Nisbet quite well. When speaking to the police and the newspapers, they referred to Nisbet as the Widdrington cashier. As their fortnightly duty always involved them leaving the train at Stannington, how would they knew which stop Nisbet travelled to unless they had spoken to him on occasion?

Justice

The third question we asked was how there could have been just one man in the compartment with Nisbet at Heaton, if there were two killers? Hall and Spink had to underline the idea of a lone gunman. If Cicely Nisbet had seen two men with her husband at Heaton, then the entire plan would have been flawed. The idea of Hall, looking out of the window, actually reinforced Cicely's testimony and he could use his presence to discourage other passengers from travelling in his compartment and act as look-out so that if anyone did enter the compartment Nisbet and Spink were in, the planned attack could be aborted. Their alibi would depend on the suggestion that Hall and Spink were always in the same compartment, next to the one that Nisbet travelled in.

The fourth question was why had no one else entered Nisbet's compartment between Heaton and Stannington. This has already been explained. Hall acted as look-out. The signal that all was well and that the plan could go ahead was him entering the compartment, at Plessey.

The fifth question, the identification evidence of Wilson Hepple, has been covered. He may have been mistaken. He may have come forward for the reward. He may even have assisted a relative. Whatever the truth is, his testimony alone was certainly not enough to determine Dickman's guilt. This has also covered the sixth question: why did Hepple not come forward until the Sunday?

The seventh question was when and why the bag was placed down the Isabella shaft. If we are correct in stating that Hall and Spink are the killers then this is no longer a mystery. It was placed down the shaft well after Dickman was in custody. It may possibly have been in the hope that it would be found and thus further incriminate Dickman, or it might have been that by this time, Hall and Spink thought that they were now completely safe and it didn't matter what happened to it.

The eighth question referred to the test firing of a gun on 4 March. It is true that Dickman might have been on that train on that date, but so too could either Hall or Spink. Friday, 4 March, would have been a day on which they, once again, made the trip to the Netherton colliery with their wage bags.

The ninth question was why did the police apparently assist with Hall's identification? Some writers have suggested a conspiracy between the police and the judiciary. That is possible but unlikely. Much more likely is a single rogue officer who, as soon as Dickman was taken to the police station, had become convinced of his guilt and wished to help things along. It does not need to be anything more sinister than this. That police officer could have had no idea that he was actually helping the real murderers.

The final question was did the idea of two killers make at least as much sense as Dickman acting alone. We have seen that it does. It actually makes much more sense and, had the police stayed with their original assumption, that two people were responsible for the murder, then the real killers might have been discovered.

John Innes Nisbet was murdered by being shot in the head five times. If the suggestion of Percival Harding Hall and John William Spink as the killers is correct then, in effect, John Alexander Dickman was also murdered by the same two individuals, by being hanged for a crime he did not commit.

Dickman's last words in court were 'I declare to all men I am innocent.' Some of his final words in a letter to his wife, penned the night before his execution, were that one day something would come to light to show that he was innocent of the crime which claimed his life.

That day has come, and it is time that the Court of Appeal took another look at the conviction of an innocent man.

Index

Anderson, Thomas, 5, 31, 45
Athey, John, 25, 33, 53, 57

Badcock, John Dennis, 59
Boland, Dr Robert, 58, 135–6
Bruce, Andrew, 10, 14, 28, 33, 53–4, 180
Burnham, Dr Charles Clarke, 3, 34, 55–6, 128–32, 135

Charlton, Thomas William, 2–3, 13, 33, 54, 135
Christie, Frank, 60, 120
Churchill, Winston, 87, 93, 149–50
Clark, Edward, 93
Cohen, Herman, 163–7
Cohen, Samuel, 58–9, 119
Condor, 142–50
Cosher, John Thomas,, 33, 55
Craig, Thomas, 26–7, 35, 41–2

Dickenson, Walter Henry, 44
Dickman, Annie, 18–19, 24, 29, 43, 83, 94, 97, 120–3, 136, 151

Dovecot Colliery, 25, 45, 54, 70–1, 103, 126, 152, 174

Elliott, Edwin, 25, 40, 137
Ellis, John, 97–100

Gosforth Police Station, 21, 24, 55, 60
Grant, John, 10, 12, 28, 33, 44, 56, 175

Hall, Percival Harding, 5–6, 16, 28, 31–2, 43, 47–51, 66, 83, 88, 103, 105, 108, 113–15, 138–9, 170–2, 175–88
Henderson, Thomas William, 26–7, 35, 41
Hepple, Wilson, 15, 17, 20, 27–8, 31, 43, 46–7, 103–104, 109, 116–17, 138, 170–3, 181–3, 187
Hogg, William, 25–6, 34, 54, 70, 103, 174
Hymen, Henrietta, 33, 57, 66, 133

Isabella Mine & Pit Shaft,
    37–40, 44, 108–109, 124–6,
    139, 183–4, 187

Kirkwood, Andrew Craig, 34,
    58, 133

Legal Personnel
    Alverstone, Lord, Lord Chief
        Justice, 87–9
    Atkinson, Edward Tindal, 43,
        44, 69, 69, 73–4
    Coleridge, Lord Justice, 43,
        68, 76–80
    Grantham, Mister Justice, 41
    Lawrence, Mister Justice, 87
    Lowenthal, Charles
        Frederick, 43
    Mitchell-Innes, Edward
        Alfred, 43, 45, 48–52,
        74–5, 112, 122
    Percy, Lord Justice William,
        43, 62
    Phillimore, Mister Justice, 87
Luard, Caroline, 150, 156–62
Luard, Charles Edward,
    156–62

Murphy, Charles Franklin,
    44, 173

Newcastle Gaol, 23, 29, 83, 89,
    97–8

Newcastle Streets
    Collingwood Street, 57, 59,
        118, 127
    Gallowgate, 15–16
    Groat Market, 57, 133
    Heaton Road, 3, 9
    Lily Avenue, 18, 20, 34, 102,
        118, 133
    Northumberland Street, 54,
        59, 102, 119, 151, 182
    Pilgrim Street, 23, 32, 55,
        88, 128
Newcastle United FC, 26, 36
Newspapers
    Daily News, 150
    Illustrated Chronicle, 47, 94
    *Manchester Sporting
        Chronicle*, 151
    The People, 166
Nisbet, Cicely, 4, 9, 14–15,
    21, 30, 35–6, 52, 83, 88,
    104–105, 109, 115, 138,
    175–6, 183, 185, 187
Norman, Clarence Henry, 149–50

Paisley, Thomas, 60
Pape and Company, Gunsmiths,
    57–8, 121, 133
Pilgrim Street Police Station, 88
Police Officers
    Bolton, Superintendent, 3
    Fullerton, Chief Constable
        James, 24

Index

Irving, Inspector James, 60
Nisbet, Constable George, 8, 33
Marshall, Superintendent Thomas, 58
Tait, Detective Inspector Andrew, 20–1, 33, 54, 66
Weddell, Superintendent John, 20–3, 27, 33, 55

Railway Stations
  Alnmouth, 2–3, 14, 33
  Heaton, 4, 30, 52, 84, 104, 128, 138, 175, 177, 179, 187
  Longhirst, 33, 53
  Morpeth, 10, 23, 25, 40, 43–4, 53, 57, 70–1, 102, 105–106, 126, 128, 175, 183–4, 186
  Newcastle Central, 2–3, 6, 44, 46, 102, 104, 108, 127, 173, 175, 182
  Stannington, 6, 11, 23, 40, 45, 48, 51, 53, 70, 73, 103, 105–106, 128, 152, 172, 175–181, 184, 186–7
Ramsay, Mark Watson, 44

Raven, Charles, 6, 16, 27, 31, 43, 46, 103, 108, 112–13, 138, 170–1, 181
Rayne and Burn Co Ltd, 4–5, 9, 85
Richardson, Elizabeth, 141–2

Sanderson, William Stafford, 25–7, 40, 137
Sedcole, Robert, 60
Simpson, Thomas, 34, 57, 127–8
Spink, John William, 5–6, 16, 23, 28, 33, 48, 51–2, 105, 109, 111–12, 138, 170, 172, 175–88
Spooner, Peter, 37–9, 58, 125–6, 139, 142
Stewart, Alice Mary, 156–7
Sweeny, Roberts, 58

Warbrick, William, 100
Wilkinson, Robert, 3, 28, 54
Willis, William, 99
Wilson, John Bradshaw, 5, 33, 45
Woodcock, Edward, 98

Yeoman, George, 53